For Monica, who else?

Us with Us

Barcelona INK, Vallespir 171, Local B, 08014 Barcelona.
ISBN: 978-1-5272-5799-3

Us with Us

Cadaqués

It all happened,
but it might not be true

Ryan Chandler
Illustrations: Javier Aznarez

Barcelona INK Books

Us with Us

Author's note,

That Cadaqués is in Catalonia, I am sure. Whether Catalonia is a region of Spain, or a nation in its own right, is less clear. But it is a place with a long history and a fierce sense of identity, not unlike Cadaqués.

That Catalonia is my wife's homeland and the place I have lived for 30 years are objective facts. Whether or not Catalonia is my home is a more subjective matter. But it is somewhere I have come to love, not unlike Cadaqués.

On October 1st, 2017, contrary to the rulings of the Spanish constitutional court, the Catalan government held an 'unauthorized' referendum on secession from Madrid.

The police brutality that day made global news. For 12 hours the world watched, slack-jawed, as voters were pulled screaming from polling booths.

In the days that followed, Catalonia infamously declared an independence which lasted all of eight seconds. The world's shortest-lived republic. Its leaders paid a high price for this chimera. Many were subsequently arrested on charges of rebellion and imprisoned. Others managed to escape. President Carles Puigdemont ran to Belgium.

Ominously, the first two arrests were of the civic leaders Jordi Sanchez and Jordi Cuixart (referred to here as JC). One was the president of a pro-independence pressure group, the other, the head of a Catalan cultural association. The message was clear.

For months, protests seemed to be routine. The noise was relentless. The yellow ribbon soon became the established symbol of support for the *presos politics*, political prisoners.

During some of that time, I escaped with my wife to this much-painted seaside town on the Costa Brava where we sheltered from the storm. I mused over pirates. She collected pebbles. And I wrote this book, a scrapbook-diary about the village, its history, some of its people and a smidgen about myself. It's not about Catalonia or politics, but when you're standing next to a bonfire, smoke inevitably gets in your eyes.

Cadaqués. 767.8 kilometres from Madrid. A place where the people talk salty, and the trees are bent double by the wind.

One road in. Same road out. Us with us.

'I've always lived learning from my master of aesthetics: Cadaqués; and it's difficult because Cadaqués seldom speaks, and when she does, she speaks Greek.'

– *Salvador Dalí*

'For centuries the only way in or out of Cadaqués was the sea. You can only understand its history and the way it is, if you consider it an island.'

– *Josep Pla*

Results of the 'illegal' referendum on Catalan independence in Cadaqués, Oct 1st, 2017.

Participation 71.18%

In favour: 1,113 (92.5%)
Against: 60 (4.9%)
Spoiled ballots: 4 (1.1%)
Null: 18 (1.5%).

'The hairpin bends on the way down are some of the sharpest I've ever driven, and if any idiot in a convertible thinks he's going to squeeze past me on a turn, he'll be fish food before you can say petrol cap.'

– *The mad bus driver*

Us with Us

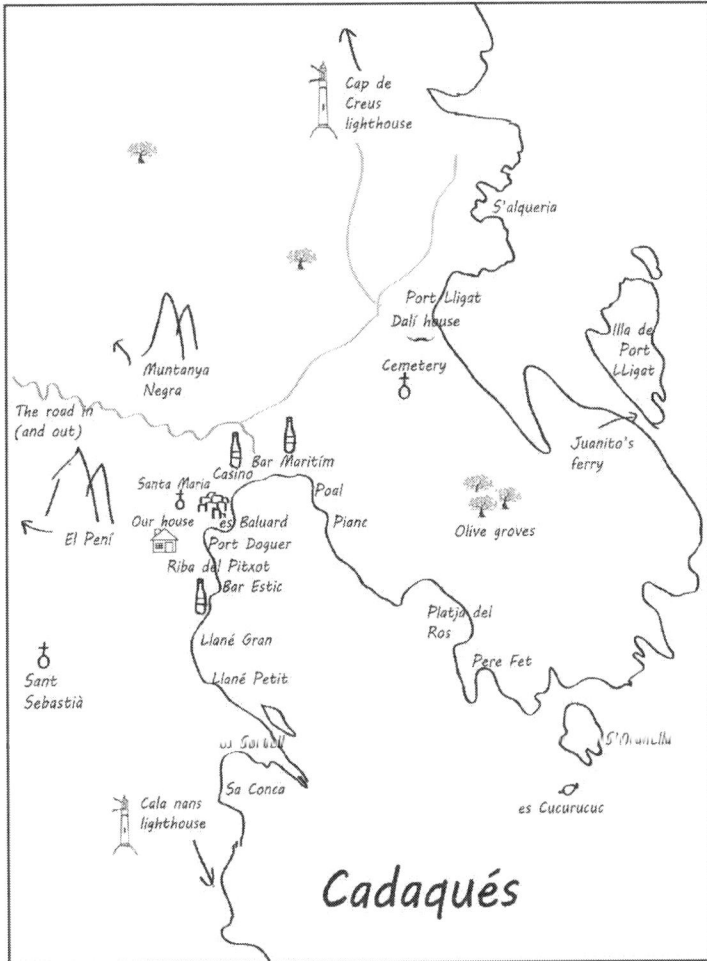

Cap de
Creus
lighthouse

S'alqueria

Port Lligat
Dalí house

Illa de
Port
LLigat

Muntanya
Negra

Cemetery

The road in
(and out)

Juanito's
ferry

Bar Marítim

Casino

Santa Maria

Poal

El Pení

Our house

es Baluard

Piano

Olive groves

Port Daguer

Riba del Pitxot

Bar Estic

Llané Gran

Platja del
Ros

Pere Fet

Sant
Sebastià

Llané Petit

es Sortell

S'Oranella

Sa Conca

es Cucurucuc

Cala nans
lighthouse

Cadaqués

Us with Us

Intro

When I first visited Cadaqués in Easter '91, I was a full-lipped long-haired youth just three days past my 24th birthday. I'd arrived in the village soaked after hitching down the coast in a cloudburst. At the time I was feeling guilty about having cheated on my girlfriend and the rain felt like penance. Or at least that's what my emotional memory tells my middle-aged self. There is no mention of it in my diary. The diary just reads:

> Hitched down with an Andalusian fisherman. Understood one word in twenty. The ride was incredible. Across the rugged cape with its bendy road and mountain curves. Dipped down into the tranquil whitewashed haven of Cadaqués. A beautiful bay with rico (sic) villas lining its tips, along with assorted palm trees and outcrops of rocks. I am in constant awe. Everything here is more. Including the prices – which I don't mind because I'm free. I don't have any money.

Funny how we choose to remember. Maybe the rain had been the day before.

Twenty-seven years later and I am married to that girlfriend and have two grown-up kids. The clipped prose of my twenties has been replaced by journalese, semi-colons, occasional poetry and an apparently defective memory. My scribblings about Cadaqués would now probably read something like this:

> Nestling between the rocky headlands of Cap de Norfeu and Cap de Creus and flanked by mountains

11

– notably the omnipresent humpbacked whale of El Pení (605m) – Cadaqués, with its white fishermen's cottages huddled around the church and pebbled coves peppering the bay, is known as the pearl of the Costa Brava.

After a dramatic history including pirates, pestilence and plague, battling dioceses, legendary generals and mass emigration to the Americas, the place has long since settled into a distinctly bohemian-chic groove. It has become a meeting point for artists, intellectuals, and free spirits.

Yawn.

But yes! It is the kind of place drifters get very seriously washed up in and the rich get very casually dressed up in.

If I had realized that in '91, I might have drifted in and got washed up myself. As it was, I hadn't, and I didn't. And back then, I had no idea the place was such a Mecca for artists either.

Not just the ubiquitous Salvador Dalí (the Willy Wonka of the Cadaqués art scene), but Pablo Picasso, Henri Matisse, Richard Hamilton, Marcel Duchamp, and David Hockney all washed up here. Sometimes with surprising results. Duchamp gave up on art and spent most of his time playing chess with the locals, Hockney left the place in tears after a shoreline bust-up with his boyfriend, and Hamilton teamed up with Dieter Roth to organize an exhibition for dogs.

It is this quirky mix of boho legend and exclusive geography that exercises such a pull – we have since visited dozens of times – and although the days when Dalí could be spotted in the Meliton Café are long gone, the charm remains. Incredibly, and against all the odds, the place has managed to retain its unlikely air of 'nothing-ever-happens-here-but-this-is-where-it's-happening'.

It is an expensively desirable piece of mind.

But now I am a thin-lipped short-haired man, a few months past my 50th birthday. I have a little money. I want to surprise the wife.

Oh, that rain...

Cadaqués. Cap de Creus. North by northeasterly, three. Visibility, moderate. Rising slowly.

Sugar on my tongue.

OCTOBER 7,2017

Hey Pep, hope you are well in these heady times. Quick question...do you still rent out that place near the beach in in Port Doguer? *15:41*

Yes. Why? *15.45*

Well, I'm looking for somewhere for a year-long lease. A present for Monica's 50th... *15:46*

http://www.airbnb.es/rooms/123946 location=Cadaqués? *15:46*

Looks amazing. What's the chance of a deal on the rent? I can pay cash if that helps you adjust the price... *15:52*

I think I can work something out. When would you want to start? *16.02*

Dunno, December 1st I suppose. The place is usually closed in November, right? *16.05*

That's when I like it! Give me a while and I'll send you a mail. *16.04*

OK but her birthday is in two weeks! *16.04*

Don't worry. Speak soon. A hug. *16.08*

Winter

Us with Us

Night, and the bay is full of fallen stars,
a huge silvered shoal, shimmering in the deep.

December 16.

Chilling

The third coldest December weekend in thirty-six years. Not as cold as the first weekend we came though. That was the coldest on record. Then, the inexorable Tramuntana was blowing a wind chill factor of −4 direct from the North Pole, accelerating over the Apennines, and straight into our bedroom. Monica slept in a onesy of a giraffe. The heads of our toothbrushes froze overnight. My pen was benumbed. And our spectacular rooftop view of the slate green sea from Port Doguer wasn't enough to fend off a nagging sensation of misgiving.

A year-long lease on a beach-side maisonette in Catalonia's swankiest seaside town for Monica's 50th? A faux demonstration of bourgeois possibility? A loving gift? Or a present for myself?

George Monbiot says second homeowners are the most selfish of people and although we are renting, and I'm not quite sure we can afford it, it is still a niggle. As for self-interested generosity, I've never bought into that adage about people always giving others things they want for themselves. It would imply that over the last twenty years I've had a strong urge to dress in fluffy pink socks and drink sweet sherry. But there's no doubt I am going to enjoy this largesse, and right now those misgivings are more to do with the dodgy carpentry of Catalan beach apartments and an absence of central heating than any fleeting philosophical quandaries.

The top floor of the apartment has a terrace by the kitchen which looks like it was fashioned by a JCB taking a chunk out of the roof. The windows must have been fixed by the builders trying to get out of its way. They whistle and rattle in the slightest breeze.

In the bedroom below, the mixed heating/air-con unit is attached to the ceiling above the bed. But heat rises. When the temperature is below freezing, the bed is still in Greenland.

So, we returned. Armed with bubble wrap, Teflon tape, oil radiators and hot water bottles. The outlook has improved but it still feels as cold as Christmas on your own. That said, at least the quietening blanket of village life has helped muffle the incessant noise that has been coming out of the Catalan airwaves and social media channels for the last few months.

Exciting times became stressing times after Catalonia's nationalists managed to convince a lot of people, myself included, that a social and national revolution was within touching distance. Spain quickly, and brutally, reminded them that large states (especially ones with dictatorial tics and a history of internecine conflict) do not allow themselves to be dismembered easily, if at all.

So I killed Twitter, ignored Facebook, and left the din behind. Exchanged it for a murmur.

Here in Cadaqués, posters in favour of the political prisoners hang from some of the pretty bougainvillea balconies and the now familiar vindicatory yellow ribbons decorate the bridge over the storm drain. But overall, the conversations you tend to hear are about the wind, weather and waves, or if Lluís and Núria are coming up for the long weekend.

Yesterday evening, as the blanket of darkness settled on this tiny town, I held hands with Monica on the seafront and watched a middle-aged lady in a black body-length bubble coat and oversized purple-framed glasses decorate a Christmas tree by the Patisserie Mallorquina. Those yellow ribbons had replaced the customary baubles.

The Patisserie Mallorquina is the same patisserie where the poet Federico Garcia Lorca used to go nuts for a puff-pastry fish with a glazed cherry eye and filled with cream. The summer of '27 when he was going nuts for Dalí. The same place Senyor Cabrisas invented the famous sweet and spongy *taps de Cadaqués*.

Perhaps the lady in the bubble coat is his granddaughter.

Cabrisas, I mean. Lorca had no kids and was infamously shot by the fascists in '36. By then, all that remained of his time in Cadaqués was the bittersweet mess of memory and a handful of poems.

Despite the encroaching icy darkness, the lady in the bubble coat seemed to have all the time in the world as she stood there and nattered to her neighbour about sweaters.

Slowly and methodically she entwined the ribbons. Over and over. One knot, then another. Gold on green.

She could have been knitting.

Knit one, pearl one.

Slip one together.

It's a wintry kind of calm.

JC in prison pending trial, 71 days.

Us with Us

Census

2,794 inhabitants
pretty much 50/50,
women and men.

26 hotels,
over a thousand beds,
1 campsite, 600 tents.

1131 first homes
40% rent
60% owned.

25km squared
some rocks some sand
7 hectares of arable land.

34ha of olive trees
11 of vine, 33 birds,
innumerable bees

69 cows...and rabbits?
There are two.
It's true.

Data taken from the Cadaqués census
as published by the local council in 2018.

Gaul

It is not unusual for nations or whole regions to have a marked character or a quirky dialect. Less so, a village. Then again, it's pretty uncommon for the people in that village to be required to surrender all the heads of the dolphins caught in county waters to the local gentry. Even in the Dark Ages.

What was it about the nobility back then and eating heads? Pigs' heads, calves' heads, lambs' heads …but dolphins, really?

Unusual, too, for a feudal hamlet to be freed from general military obligations. In 1280, Ponç Hug, the Count of Empúries (could there ever be a more phonetically appropriate name for a Count?) confirmed that the *Cadaquesencs* would not be obliged to leave the village to form part of an army and were only duty-bound to defend the village itself.

Imagine how a law like this might have changed the history of Europe!

The strategic importance of Cadaqués cannot be underestimated. In the days before road, a deep natural port on the Western Mediterranean coast was like having an extra arrow in your quiver. The Counts of Empúries and the Benedictine monks who power-shared the peasants at the time were keen to keep it in their hands. The French and the Corsairs were just as keen to take it away from them. Hence the need to defend the village.

The years of continual conflict forged a notable spirit among the villagers. They gained a reputation. They were hard as nails.

21

Outside of the pages of *Asterix and Obelix*, or the occasional episode of *Vikings* on HBO, it's also rare to find small fishing villages willing to take on the might of battleships.

In 1623 when the galleon *Sant Maurici* entered the bay on its way back from Genoa, the soldiers were causing trouble of the rowdiest kind (long journey, too much rum, not enough sex, Friday night) when the locals began to stone them. The soldiers opened fire. Some children were injured. The revolt was so intense the soldiers almost had to leave swimming back to the galleon. A few weeks later, the *Sant Maurici* returned, set on revenge and punishment. The response from the locals was, again, so virulent, the galleon had to retire to nearby Port Lligat before sailing back down the coast to Palamós with its rudder firmly between its sails.

Jeroni Pujades, a chronicler of the times, said the *Cadaquesencs* were 'the most villainous and uncouth people on the whole coast. Barbarous and possessing of no other reason other than 'we don't want you and we don't want to be wanted.'

If the town were to have a coat of arms, the motto would be *Nos amb Nos*: Us with Us.

It doesn't. But the motto lives.

JANUARY 19, 2018

Rain. 80kmh wind. minus 7 feel bad factor. *16.04*

Just got a windproof, fluffy fleece tracksuit *16.05*

Nothing will scare me *16.05*

And got a Ryan blanket for the night *16.05*

Did you get the bus tickets? *16.06*

Yep. But I reckon it'll be empty. Who'd go up in this weather? Unless they were mad… *16.07*

> A thin broth simmers on the stove,
> the windows are steamed up with condensation.

January 20.

Barking

Sometimes I wonder about my sanity. Although I'm not as bonkers as the bus driver who drove us up last night.

He spent the whole time talking to himself, muttering under his breath and then played chicken all the way down the road into the bay with its terrifying bends.

It's blisteringly cold, windy and miserable. Monica is exhausted and needs her lie-ins. And I'm on the spectrum when it comes to taking part in group activities. So why get up at 7.30am and climb a nasty steep path for an hour to stand around eating crappy sandwiches and watch the villagers get drunk, feast on sea urchins, and slap each other senseless?

And yet, that is exactly what we did.

Almost.

Sebastian is the patron saint of the village and every year on January 20th, the locals scale the mountain to the nearby hermitage of Sant Sebastià to celebrate. The enclave, a tiny chapel and not so tiny house some fifteen hundred feet above the village, was sold to the Guinness family years ago. The story has it that Jonathan Guinness pipped Salvador Dalí to the post by a couple of months. The exclusive off-the-beaten-track pad is the perfect getaway for eccentric millionaires. It's easy to see why they both wanted it.

Our landlord's wife Mercè, who we occasionally hike with, had told us about the event. She also mentioned that the place was up for sale again (a cool couple of million, I'll bet).

What she didn't mention was that neither she nor Pep would be going. That every year on the morning of the festival, a convoy drove up carrying barbecues, musicians, the ancients and the priest. Or, that the rest of the villagers met in front of the Casino before setting off.

So, we just walked up on our own. Meh.

The program said 9.45 at the top for bell ringing and 11 o'clock mass, followed by dancing, eating and debauchery.

We were early.

The place was deserted. The house was eerily closed so we had a nose around. What a place! Set in a sloping olive grove, the white-washed cottage with light blue shutters was smaller than I'd expected and attached to the side of the chapel like an afterthought. It had amazing views over Cadaqués, the cape, and its two lighthouses. It also had a huge swimming pool (currently full of green slime).

We sat on a bench by the pool, zipped up our jackets, pulled our hats down over our ears and opened the flask of tea. If only for the panoramic views, the climb would have been worth it, but it wasn't long before we heard the shouts and laughter of people making their way up the mountainside. Unsure of feast day etiquette, we went back to the edge of the olive grove and waited.

Bon dia, a nod, another *bon dia*, and another, and another. Soon there were hundreds of people clambering up the little paths and through the trees. A mix of weather-beaten young men in cagoules and jeans, well-heeled ladies in fashionista-

25

leggings, and a scramble of scruffy kids. On the other side of the house, cars were arriving with the oldies and the entertainment.

How had they timed that?

And then it all kicked off.

People were soon setting up foldable tables and chairs, mounting barbecues, and a group of musicians began to set up by the house.

When it came time for mass, the bells rang out, but it was clear that most of the people wouldn't fit in the chapel. It was also clear that half the people weren't bothered. Just like normal life at the bottom of the hill.

I wasn't too bothered either, but I was keen to see the inside of the chapel.

It was surprisingly ornate. An elaborate dark chandelier, bereft of the candles, hung in the nave. The altar was four marble columns with gold leaf embellishment and what looked like a portable Jesus on a cross. Maybe the priest takes it with him to these sporadic out-of-town raves.

After mass – a sedate mumbling affair followed by a short hymn – the brass band picked up the pace outside and small groups began to dance *sardanes*. Flumes of smoke began to rise from the barbecues between the olive trees. The party was in full swing.

We ate our sad Philadelphia sandwiches and stayed on the margins, watching as people grilled sausages and lamb chops. One group had a bucket of sea urchins which they ate straight from the shells with teaspoons. Another passed around a *porró* of red wine which they drank flamboyantly, arms outstretched, the arc cascading into their mouths and splashing over their chins.

Looking at the smoky woodland party, the improbable image of a picnic in a Narnian forest sprang to mind. More so when an old man wearing a traditional gnomish *barretina* started to organize a funny circle dance and chant, *'i si el Peret no vol ballar, garrotades, garrotades'* ('if Peret doesn't want to dance, bash him with a stick'), at which point everyone started slapping each other on the back and laughing. Sometimes the slapping was quite violent. The harder the slap, the louder the laugh.

Suddenly, and unexpectedly, Monica jumped up and joined in the *patocada*. Almost simultaneously, a toothless old man with a nasty twitch nudged me, grinned, and offered me a swig from his *porró*.

'No t'animes, noi?'... Not gonna give it a go, lad?

I took a swig of the wine, a rough garnatxa. *'Gracies, sí, i no, gracias.'*

We had both clearly walked through the wardrobe.

Well, actually, Monica had walked through the wardrobe.

To be honest, I was still peeping through the coats.

JC in prison pending trial, 106 days.

Eating Urchins

Here's an outrageously tenuous segue. Jacobus Voragine in *The Golden Legend* says of the slaughter of Sebastian, 'the archer shot at him till he was as full of arrows as an urchin.' The time for eating urchins in the Empordà is January/February. The apex of this culinary season, particularly popular in Cadaqués, must surely be January 20th. Seb's Saint's day.

The fact that Saint Sebastian is the patron saint of the town, or that the renowned chef Ferran Adrià invented his famous dish of white bean foam and sea urchin just around the corner in Cala Montjoi, just add salt and pepper to this spiky concoction of coincidence.

The commercial fishing of urchins is strictly prohibited around Cadaqués but there are a limited number of licences given out to private individuals during this period, and although urchins do occasionally appear in the fishmonger's, it's unusual.

I suppose, if you were keen, you could probably risk a fine and hypothermia by having a quick winter dip and picking one for yourself. Just don't get greedy. And beware of the spines, they can sting like hell.

There's no secret to eating them. No special preparation needed. Only the roe is eaten, the five tiny orange tongues inside.

To pull the roe out, simply turn over the urchin, cut a circle around the top by its mouth, rinse it in the same sea water you pulled it from, and then carefully eat it with a teaspoon.

The taste is like seawater with extra umami and a melt-in-your-mouth texture somewhere between a soft-boiled egg and foie gras.

Not for everyone. I thought they were a bit icky.

But some say they are exquisite.

You might say, almost saintly...

Phil

By the end of the 1700s, Cadaqués was buzzing. And it wasn't the bees.

A poor fishing village was slowly becoming a prosperous community of sailors and sea captains trading across the Mediterranean.

Following the abolition in 1778 of the monopolies on trade with the Americas held by Seville and Cadiz, the world's oceans opened up. A golden age of sail and commerce coincided with a thriving wine trade. The terraced hillsides were resplendent with vines and the *Cadaquesencs'* cups rannneth over.

In the early 1800s it was boom-town. Just the barrels needed for the salted fish and wine sparked a whole industry in itself: importing the carefully treated wood and then working it into the curved slats of the *doga* was big business. Soon a small village grew into a small town. There was a chocolate factory, a linen factory, wineries, warehouses... a population of nearly 3,000. But still no road. Import-export was strictly maritime.

Then disaster struck. Only a couple of decades before they would finally manage to get that road, the Philloxera got there first and wiped out the vines.

Philloxera (/fɪˈlɒksərə/; from Ancient Greek: φύλλον, leaf, and ξηρός, dry), also known as the pesky moth.

As a result, by the turn of the century, more than half the population sailed off to Cuba and the Americas.

Cadaqués was forced to reinvent itself.

It became a smugglers' paradise.

Following the chaos of the Carlist wars in the mid-19th century (trendsetters in Spain's interminable history of civil strife), the scarcity of goods such as silk, tobacco and sugar coupled with the village's isolated position and its plethora of secret coves made it a haven for contraband.

Once regularly sacked by pirates, including the notorious Red Beard whose burning down of the local church in 1543 went pre-Renaissance viral, the pillaged were now forced to become kinds of pirates themselves. Gamekeepers turned poachers.

Their nearest neighbours referred to the *Cadaquesencs* as *tabaquers, contrabandistes, bons mariners i lladres*: tobacco hawkers, smugglers, good sailors and thieves.

Meanwhile, some of the emigrants known as *Indians*, began to return home. Their pockets full of freshly minted Cuban cash. They had struck gold in tobacco and sugar and, yes, if not directly involved in the slave trade, that gold was often made on the back of slave labour.

Many of these *Indians* (the lucky few) used their new-found wealth to build some of the more ostentatious mansions that can be seen around the village, like the modernista Casa Serinyana (also known as Casa Blava) and what is now the Casino on the seafront.

This Americas-Cuba-Cadaqués connection is celebrated every June during the *Festa dels Indians*.

Spain lost Cuba in 1898 after a brief war with the USA. The war, sparked by a suspect explosion in a US warship (CIA tactics pre-CIA?), signalled the end of one empire and the beginning of another.

31

And the only territory of any value that Spain had left was Catalonia.

Portside, moonless bitumen sea
a school of sloops brood in the jug.

February 2.

Flagging

December and January flew by in a freeze. We spent Christmas back in the UK and since then the temperature has been ossifying. We have come three times in the last two months. A worse ratio than our middle-ageing sex life. The bubble wrap was fun though.

Tonight, is the anniversary of the big chill. On this day 60 years ago, a cold snap killed off most of the village's olive trees. After an unseasonably warm patch of weather, the temperature dropped 42°C. It was 12 degrees below zero. The Tramuntana was blowing 75kmh. Accounting for wind chill factor, it was 32 below zero. The water in the villagers' *dolls* turned to ice. And the olive trees died. Frozen solid.

The only thing (apart from fishing and smuggling) that had permitted the villagers to struggle through the scarcity of the Franco post-war years, was gone. The old spectral photographs of frozen sea spray from that day after are eerily beautiful, but the destruction was brutal. 500 olive groves lost.

Fortunately for Monica and myself, I think this is the warmest night we've had yet. Still cold though.

The Casino, where I'm writing this, is as dead as school on Sunday, like elsewhere in Catalonia. And the 'Casino'? It isn't a gambling den, but a bar and local hub. The inscription over the door reads *Societat l'Amistat* - Society of Friends.

Tonight, though, it's just a couple of old guys at the bar. A television chattering away in the corner to no-one in particular. Scores of empty wooden chairs waiting for the game.

The yellow ribbons are everywhere now. Spreading from the bridge like contagious party decorations: from the local council steps to the walkway of the bus station, no handrail is safe. The festive protest theme continues on the village's L-shaped lampposts which are bedecked with miniature *Estelades*, the Catalan republican flag. It's is a good fit for Cadaqués. The white star on a blue background next to the red and yellow stripes was inspired by the Cuban flag, and the two places share common history.

But I fear these mini military standards will not survive the winter. Many are already fraying. Soaked by the salty sea spray and battered by the Tramuntana. Others curl around the streetlights, clinging on in the face of the onslaught.

Cadaqués may be one of the points in Catalonia furthest from Madrid (about 800km via the A2), but even here, in the long evenings and darkened porches of the closed-up restaurants, what might usually just be out-of-season melancholy smells of the retreat blues.

And it's no joke. The political fallout is taking its toll on the natives. A recent article in the Spanish newspaper *ABC,* titled 'sick of the *procés*' claimed that Catalan chemists were running out of natural anti-depressants like valerian root, and quoted local doctors as saying there had been an increase in visits from people with sleep disorders. The Catalan department of health has even released a video telling the general population to 'limit their access to news to no more than twice a day, and work on their sense of humour.' You couldn't make it up.

Earlier, at dusk in the main square, just along from the gnarled pokeweed trees with their leafless black branches cupped like zombie hands to the sky, I noticed that one of the two enormous cypresses was full of swifts. A whole parliament of them chattering away. The chorus was deafening.

When the church bell rang for evening mass, they ignored it and chirped on regardless. It rang again, more like a warning of imminent invasion than evensong (I am going to have to investigate that bell tower's repetitive tic), and the birds just seemed to get louder.

I imagined them to be arguing heatedly about something, perhaps discussing the merits of the flags and ribbons.

Monica said it was the mosquito hour and they were just over excited.

I wondered why they had chosen that particular tree, and not the other. Or why they hadn't opted for a comfier berth in one of the warmer trees in the centre of the village.

The flags are holding up a little better there, away from the sea and sheltered from the wind. Those *Estelades* will probably make it through to Spring.

The ferocity of the Iberian summer sun is another matter entirely.

JC in prison pending trial, 169 days.

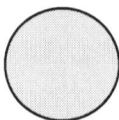

La Gritta. (1)

Number 28 of 92 restaurants in Cadaqués

Joe90
Chicago
👍52

'Thank God!'

When we drove into Cadaqués it was a Friday night around 10. It was like a ghost town. Even the gas station was closed. What do these guys do if they run out of gas?? I thought we'd made a mistake. I mean this place is in all the guidebooks and we kinda expected a bit more life. Then we saw La Gritta! Thank God!

There were only a couple of places open to eat and this one was the only one with any clients. It was almost lively. You could see most of them were from around here and knew the place, so we guessed it must be OK.

We had some tasty fish soup and some grilled squid with a carafe of red wine. Came to about 60 dollars for the three of us. Cool.

Maybe better times to visit Cadaqués though.

92 restaurants? Not in February man!

Date of visit: February, 2018

Good vibrations

Inspiration for artists, recreation for dropouts, ideal location for sailors, and pole of attraction for tourists. Cadaqués is a magnet. But why?

The beaches are rubbish, the light is better in Nice, they had to rebuild the mountainsides with dry stone wall terraces to cultivate vines. There is nowhere to cultivate crops, no good supply of drinking water. It's bumpy, and a bit too big for its boots. Even when sacked by pirates, pummelled by pestilence and priced out by Engel &Volkers, they keep coming back for more. So, what is going on?

To get to the root cause you have to dig down deep, literally.

Telluric currents are phenomena observed in the Earth's crust and mantle. These geomagnetically induced currents, caused by solar winds and the magnetosphere, are particularly strong in Cadaqués.

Basically, the place makes you feel good. It has good vibes.

Better still, these vibes result from both natural *and* human activity. While the dramatic drop of the mountains into the sea might account for half the magic energy floating around Cadaqués, the continual thrum of shiny happy people is its own self-fulfilling prophecy.

There are several telluric currents – orographic lines – detectable in Cadaqués. One runs down from the Pení towards the sea and the cliffs of Punta Prima. Another from Puig de ses Formigues and out to the lighthouse, sinking into the sea by the island of Massa d'Ors, the final point of force of the Pyrenees.

Don't believe it?

37

Just get out your pendulum and watch it spin.

What's more, the whole area is peppered with dolmens. Including Catalonia's finest specimen, the Creus de Corbatella. And everyone knows that prehistoric man was pretty damn telluric when it comes to stone circles and rock formation.

And before those cavemen, when the Gods were doling out good vibrations and mountain formations for fun, Heracles passed-by this way. He came to lend Queen Pyrene a hand in her battle with King Gerion (Girona) – or rape her, depending on your politics or which story books you read. Either way, he was besotted and so aggrieved when she later died, he built her a very very big hill as a mausoleum and the Pyrenees got their name. Those very same mountains that pour down into the bay, filling it with telluric energy.

The main plot of Umberto Eco's novel *The Pendulum* revolves around the search for the *Umbilicus Mundi*, the mystic centre of the Earth which is supposed to be a certain point from where a person can control the energies and shapes of the earth, thus reforming it at will. It is here.

In Michael Houellebecq's novel *The Possibility of an Island*, it's claimed that human beings are especially sensitive to the telluric currents and that they incite sexual promiscuity.

Shadows disco, in the passage behind the seafront.

In the Waterboys' song *Don't Bang the Drum*, Mike Scott sings: 'Here we stand in a special place, what will you do here? ...here we are in a fabulous place, what are you gonna dream here?'

Dalí dreamed it.

Cadaqués has the power to make you happy.

> "'What day is it?'
> 'It's today,' squeaked Piglet.
> 'My favourite day,' said Pooh.'"

February 24.

Smiling

Despite the warm sunshine on the terrace and a lazy stroll to Puig de s'Alqueria with the sun in my eyes and my hands in Monica's. Despite the big-screen derby, the funky music and the four pints of Guinness in Can Shelabi last night. Despite the tiny waves lapping at my toes as I look out to the island of Port Lligat. Despite this long-needed but timid advance on Spring, I will not be happy until I have my 'barbecue and sardines on the beach' moment. Until I have my funny bamboo rod to catch the fish with, sitting on a small hump of rock, humming. Until I have started and finished my 100-acre-wood map of Cadaqués marked with Eeyore's special drinking hole and the secret path to Piglet's hidey hole.

Yet, like the weather, I am happier than last month. Possibly happier than most people. Certainly happier than half the planet. And definitely happier than those Catalan politicians in jail (although political martyrdom does have a perverse kind of appeal). That is a lot of happiness. But the older I get, the more I seem to suffer from OCHD. Obsessive-compulsive happiness disorder

OCHD is planning the weekends so carefully that every minute of that precious free time is used in the pursuit of pleasure. OCHD is anticipating holidays in every tiny detail to

39

ensure success and then breaking down in a square in Istanbul because the planning has failed and you are forced to improvise.

In the initial stages, it can be mistaken for choice.

Making informed decisions about television programmes or even turning off the box in favour of a good book? Early OCHD.

When you lovingly peruse that cookery book, searching out fresh herbs and unusual ingredients, dedicating hours to the titillation of your taste buds. OCHD.

If you do it for the love of your family which in turn makes you even happier. Intense OCHD, with complications.

In fact, the moment other people begin to interact with your syndrome you may need to resort to alternative therapies such as solitary walk treatment and, in extreme cases, poetry.

This is why my barbecue and fishing moment has to be so perfectly constructed. I am talking about the creation of a momentary legacy of felicity, a nirvanic shot of joy. A true and honest work of happiness performed only for the grand scheme of things. Here in Cadaqués, in the epicentre of telluric energy: Pere Fet Cove.

The light will have to be right and it is essential I catch the sardines, not carry them from the local supermarket in a tatty plastic bag.

And I'll need to learn to fish.

Tut tut. Looks like rain.

JC in prison pending trial 141 days.

Food love (1)

Ultimate Chicken Noodle Soup

When your tectonic plates are calcified
your gentle expressions are earthquake lines
when your fine bone china is swollen blue
your pianist fingers are playing the spoons,

cinnamon apple crumble.

When your swan lake sweep is turkey wattle
your flowing cups are empty bottles
when your rolling hills are quarried scree
your Flying Scotsman, stationr'y,

Otto Lengi's poached salmon and french beans,
for the vitamin E.

When your Great Ocean Road is a Sunday stroll
your festival tent is paid freehold
when your cosmic dust is iron and lead
your Papua New Guinea, a potting shed,

lemon meringue pie with crème fraîche,
in dollops.

When your stroboscope flash is a reading lamp
your puffa jacket is an eiderdown
when your poker dice is a busted flush
your ticket tout is a queue for the bus,

butternut squash ravioli, with wild rocket salad.
Pepper.

41

Us with Us

When your boogaloo bop is a shopping channel
your sequinned vest, soft check flannel
when your twist and shout is all bump and grind
your rear-view mirror is your huge behind,

quinoa and pistachio salad.
For definite.

When your Radio One is Radio Four
your high-gloss paint is a stripped-down door
when your Coach and Horses is a three-legged mare
your Louis the fifteenth, a reclining chair,

Mary Berry's strawberry pavlova.

When your birds and bees are the apples of your eye
your magic wand is a Henkel knife
when your long tall Sally is a snoring Jimmy
and your silk top hat is a kitchen pinny,

basting becomes ritual
brisket the surrender.

Ultimate chicken noodle soup.

Food love (2)

February 25.

Stewing

Today, I cooked for Monica (and myself, of course), what I thought would be a Cadaqués take on a typical Catalan dish: *suquet de peix,* fish stew. I say 'thought' because I made it up and the *escórpora* (scorpion fish) I used for the *caldo* is very common around here. The local cuisine might like to identify itself with the anchovy, but this spiky, ugly, bony, mean-looking fish is far more *Cadaquesenc* than an anchovy could ever be.

Ingredients

Extra-virgin olive oil
A few cloves of garlic, crushed.
A couple of tomatoes peeled and chopped, an onion.
Several potatoes, washed and peeled and quartered
Half a cup of dry white wine (or more) preferably Marbre or similar white from the Empordà.
1.5 cups fish stock which you made earlier using monkfish head and handful of cheap prawns or langoustines and scorpion fish.
A pinch of saffron
1 teaspoon sugar
1 kilo firm white fish fillets (such as hake, cod, halibut), cut into chunks
8 medium or large expensive prawns
Salt and pepper to taste

For the *picada*

10 raw almonds
2 large cloves of garlic, peeled
Extra-virgin olive oil
1 tablespoon chopped parsley

Instructions

Slowly heat the olive oil in wide heavy pan (a cast iron pan if possible, a clay pot would be authentically regional, but I've cracked three on the wrong heat so I'm not a fan).
Add the garlic, tomatoes and onion and sauté for 10 minutes.
Add the potatoes, wine and stock (cover the potatoes).
Add the salt and pepper, saffron and sugar.
Cover and simmer on a low heat for 20 minutes.

To prepare the *picada*, coat a small pan in olive oil and heat to medium high (don't let it burn). Add the almonds and garlic, and brown on all sides. Once cool, pulp it in your blender or in a pestle and mortar for that more authentic peasant feel. If necessary, add a bit of the stew's juice to blend.

Finally, add the fish chunks to the stew and cook for about four minutes (uncovered). Then add the prawns and cook until pink.

It was delicious. Ultimate chicken noodle soup. Well, actually, ultimate fish stew. But that doesn't scan.

JC in prison pending trial 142 days.
Porridge.

Costas

The *ley de costas* is a Spanish law which theoretically outlaws construction within 100 metres of the sea. The problem, as you can see from a quick glance at any Spanish costa, is that by the time it was passed in 1988 most of the damage had already been done and retroactive demolition was not usually part of the deal, but there were exceptions.

The over-zealous Socialist government of the time was so keen to be seen implementing the law that it tried to demolish both the Bar Maritim and Bar Boia on the town's main beach. Local opposition was fierce, and both iconic sheds were saved. The fact that a few famous artists used to have their morning coffees on the terrace was enough to sway the balance. They have since been granted the status of buildings of 'local cultural interest' and are protected by preservation orders.

Ironic, too, that much of Cadaqués' charm is down to the absence of such a law. The ramparts and some of the older parts of the village drop directly down into the sea, and those prettily piled-up houses with their hundreds of differently shaped windows present the vista for a very popular selfie. Picasso would have had to paint something entirely different in 1910. Einstein would have had to find somewhere else to play his violin.

It is the new build encroaching on virgin beaches that the law was really designed to prevent. While its success has been limited, it has helped open up new coastal paths by obliging owners to allow right of access to ramblers, swimmers and sunbathers.

Not always willingly.

I swim forever in the orange glow of my eyes shut tight.

March 9.

Trespassing

Thunder and sunshine. A rough sea. The low cloud over the Pení gives the place that enchanted mystique you see in photos of misty rainforests in *National Geographic*.

This morning I cycled up to Pere Fet Cove on the bike. Although bike is a big word for that piece of junk: a rusty foldable picked up from a second-hand shop for Tadhg's Christmas present that has a habit of folding and unfolding mid-ride.

Tadhg had refused it on the grounds that it was not a brand-new fixie. In retrospect, a sensible lad. Although I do wonder if it's a generational thing that I see all second-hand things as bathed in cool, but my kids only want bling. It's probably just me.

The perfectly formed Pere Fet is protected from the Tramuntana and the place is usually deserted first thing in the morning. Hidden away at the very tip of the bay, northside, there are many ways to arrive but the simplest and quickest is a short cut through someone else's garden. Just a quick dash through the cluster of houses tucked in behind the Platja del Ros. The only problem being that this can occasionally cause trouble with the residents.

I dropped the bike at the end of Ros and ignored the *camí privat* (private path) sign. I was verbally armed (just in case) with a diatribe about the Spanish coastal law but was swiftly disarmed by an unexpected invitation from an unexpected group breakfasting on their porch. What were they even doing there? This was a random weekend in March and *that* house was almost always empty.

At first, I couldn't make out what they were saying. In fact, I didn't want to believe they were actually shouting to me. As I was fiddling with the gate between their garden and the beach (there was a padlock), I turned to look at them, ready to hit them with full force of the law, when they decked me with the simplest of offers: 'Lovely croissants, come and join us for breakfast, why don't you? I mean you might as well now you're practically at our table!'

Irony, huh?

Eyes down, I jumped the gate into the cove.

I wish I'd had the balls to accept.

Pere Fet was empty. As I'd hoped it would be. So, I spent a soul-warming hour dancing with my shoes off and my earphones in.

The sensation was similar to what I'd felt during last night's drive in on the coach where I'd sat alone up front (the last bus from Barcelona on a Thursday is almost always deserted), watching tail-lights dancing in the motorway dark.

It was an 'I-was-quiet-now' moment. A gentle hand closing a sleeping book. Fireworks in the distance. The world driving by holding me tight.

Both beach dance and bus ride touched that soft intangible that is a good place to be, when, like me, you spend vast and unnecessary amounts of time worrying about mortality. My own, and other people's.

But especially my own.

47

Hypochondria is what differentiates us from animals.
Well, that, and the ability to pay attention to signs.
I walked back the long way round.

JC in prison pending trial, 153 days.

48

Bar Maritim

Number 43 of 92 restaurants in Cadaqués

Walkers31
York

👍 52

'Amaaazing chips'

The best *patates braves* I've ever tasted. Beautifully fried in their skins, the perfect cut, fantastic tangy sauce. Amaaaaaazing. And what a view!

Date of visit: March, 2018

Nan

The walk to the lighthouse *Far de Cala Nan* is one of the easiest and most rewarding around Cadaqués. Clearly signposted. Walking boots not required. Flip-flops problematic.

Leaving the village on the right-hand side as you look out to sea and following the road round from Llane beach, up past the hotel and the hippy commune, you first arrive at Sa Conca. Here, the mass of pebbles and stones can make both sitting and getting into the water a painful experience, but its relative seclusion and fantastic snorkelling are worth the effort if you fancy stopping.

A few years back there was a big hotel. Now it's just a pile of rubble. The story has it that some Russians bought the place, demolished it and put in plans for a glitzy casino. A real one. The local council denied planning permission. This is Cadaqués after all. And the Russians have been sulking through litigation ever since.

The road to Cala Nan continues up to the right, and after an initial steep slope past a huddle of houses, you are soon high above the bay. There are stunning views down to the village and across the whole of the Cap de Creus National Park and its scraggy coastline. On a clear day, you can see across the treacherous Gulf of Lion all the way to France.

In Spring, the barren landscape comes alive as desert figs and weaver's broom come into bloom among the juniper bushes. The proliferation of juniper bushes is said to be one of the explanations for the village's name, juniper in Catalan is *cadec*. Cadecs, Cadaqués.

Strange it doesn't have its own brand of gin, though.

At the top, a narrow path winds towards the lighthouse past ruined artillery batteries and cylindrical piles of stones. These spherical cairns look like Stone Age burial mounds or megalithic monuments, but most are simply heaps of discarded rocks from the dry-stone walling: *clopers*.

The lighthouse, a stubby white building with a marble plaque above the door, dated 1853, is a bit of an anti-climax after the spectacular highs of the walk. In the 1980s the Spanish government wanted to replace it with a metal tower, but the local council managed to stop it. The same way they managed to stop them demolishing the beach bars. Heritage is heritage. Cadaqués is Cadaqués.

It was here, in this gorse-covered moonscape, that Kirk Douglas and Yul Brynner came to film *The Light at the End of the World* in 1971. The film was based on Jules Verne's book involving piracy in the mid-19th century and inspired by the Isla de Estados near the Tierra de Fuego in Cape Horn.

Brynner was the pirate; Douglas was the lighthouse keeper. But the lighthouse wasn't the lighthouse.

Not content with the Cadaqués' actual lighthouse – too stubby – they built a proper one nearby. A tall tubular one, like the ones you see in storybooks.

And they didn't take it home with them.

It was left to ruin and didn't get cleaned up until 2006.

> All the skies the sea has drunk,
> hang dark above my head.

March 10.

Maudlin

My mood is crepuscular.

I am sitting on a rock looking out to Nan's lighthouse from Sa Conca. I'd originally planned on walking to the lighthouse but it's grey, windy and late. And I can't be bothered. So here I am on the rock. Eeyore, not Piglet. Waiting for some inspiration on this miserable afternoon.

Behind me, there's a semi-derelict whitewashed hut with closed weather-beaten green shutters. An old sandal sits in the corner on the sill. The faded pink writing above the shutters reads *refrescos, bocadillos, helados*. Refreshments, sandwiches, ice cream. It's all that's left standing of the old Rocamar Hotel.

In front of me, a small island of slate, like a shark's fin, sulks out at sea. A solitary man in a boat is laying out yellow buoys across the bay in preparation for the coming season.

And waves. Hundreds of tiny waves, breaking gently over the pebbles.

The tiny waves seem to be getting closer – although there's not much of a tide around here – and I am vaguely aware that one of them is eventually going to soak me. I don't really care though. I'm in one of those dour moods where I feel like the waves are going to get everyone in the end.

As they try to claw the pebbles back to the sea it sounds sound like applause. Over and over. Rhythmical and repetitive.

I wonder who or what they're clapping for. But wait! What's that? A tractor? What a racket! A decrepit diesel. Stinking the place out.

Strange I didn't notice that before (then again, I am a bit wrapped up in my own wanky bubble). I suppose he must have been doing some work in the rubble of the old hotel, but I haven't heard any noise. Maybe he was just sitting in the cabin looking at porn on his phone.

Whatever it is he's been doing or not doing; he's done it now. Probably signing off and going back to the Casino for an early-doors.

Seems like most of the locals go to the Casino for an early-doors, most of the time. Especially at this time of year when they are all busy preparing for Easter: building the platforms for the beach bars, cleaning windows, dusting down the restaurants. Same this year as last. Over and over.

Easter is when the outside world begins to arrive.

Yesterday on the bus I overheard two South American women, Bolivian I think, talking about how they were coming to prepare the house for the *señores* and how they would be staying on there for the rest of the season to look after the *señores*.

Like they do every year. Same this year as last. If not them then some different ladies. *Si señor, si señor.* Been going on for generations. Over and over. Some things don't change. Like the waves, wearing down the tiniest of pebbles.

Sí señor, I'd better move. It's getting dark, and my boots just got wet. Time for an early-doors.

The Casino it is.

Every cliché has a silver lining.

Postscript, March 11.

I think I just made my first friend.

I was cheering myself up in the Casino when I met Javi the painter. Late thirties, a scruffy beard, a shock of mousey brown hair, baggy jeans and a chunky cardigan. He looks like a painter. He might have even had a couple of brushes sticking out of his pocket.

He has a distinctively Edward Gorey take on the village that I like, and I've bought a couple of tiny pictures from him in the past. But when I last visited the studio he shares with Roimeser, I noticed something wasn't right. One of those subjects you're not sure you should broach. Unless, that is, it's early doors and you've had a couple. Then it doesn't matter...

'I hope you don't mind me mentioning it, but I couldn't help noticing that lately, the other guy in your studio, he seems to be copying you... a bit.'

His face lit up.

'I know, I thought that too and it's terrible, there's no one I can talk to about it. You know what it's like when you share a studio with someone...and in this village'

I didn't. But he bought me another beer.

'I got you babe, dum da da, dum da da, I got you babe...'

JC in prison pending trial, 154 days.

March 10, 2018

On the bus — 19.04

Yehhh — 19.05

It's the mad driver — 19.05

Nehhh. — 19.06

I had the mad driver too — 19.06

In Casino. With the painter. — 19.07

He drives like a loony, but I need to be at the front — 19.08

Yeh. He kept driving off the white lines on the way up. — 19.09

Put some music on and chill! — 19.09

Eiiooo — 21.08

Eiiooo — 21.11

You not answering. Have I lost you to the golden bubbles? — 21.26

'Oh my whiskers and ears, how late it's getting!'

Javier

I watched Javi exit his studio
like the White Rabbit,
an unlikely lime-green lilo
under his arm.
He was shortly followed
by his pocket-sized daughter
in a straw hat,
clutching a fishing net.

Then he was off
round the corner
quick as a brush stroke,
off the canvas
before you could say palette.
He left her quayside
skipping a song,
and chasing invisible butterflies.

Spring

Us with Us

Black Mountain

Just by the roundabout at the entrance to the village, there is a narrow set of stone steps which lead up to the Muntanya Negra (Black Mountain). The climb is punishing but in less than an hour, you can reach the peak with its panoramic views. To the south lie the plains of the Empordà. To the north, the Pyrenees and the border with France. To the east, Cadaqués and the Mediterranean. And to the west, the towering peak of Canigó and the snaking monster of the AP7 motorway.

Canigó is a major signifier in the Catalan imagination. At the summit stands a cross decorated with the Catalan flag, and on the eve of Sant Joan (June 23), a bonfire is lit on the top from which people take torches in a spectacular relay to ignite fires elsewhere around Catalonia. Imagine the Olympic torch relay reinvented as an affirmation of national identity.

Some claim that Canigó was the last resting place of Noah's ark, not Mount Ararat. Ergo, Catalonia is God's own country.

The AP7 is known as the motorway of the Mediterranean. It is also the principal route for road haulage from most of Europe to Madrid. For the last three decades it has been at the forefront of the Catalan Republican Left party's (ERC) drive for independence (sic).

ERC regularly questions why the Catalans have to pay tolls when the rest of Spain travel for free.

It is not strictly true. There are tolls in Madrid, Andalucía, the Basque Country and many other parts of Spain, if perhaps fewer of them.

Either way, thirty years ago ERC had 6 MPs in the Catalan parliament. Now it has 32. And its leader is in jail.

The AP7 is a major signifier in Catalan transportation.

Late moon, early sun,
the snow burns on the horizon.

March 28.

Mischief-making

If I had ever contemplated getting up at 3am in Cadaqués it might have been to do some night-time squid fishing on Pep's boat; my fat-cat *independentista* landlord has told me hundreds of times about his semi-illegal adventures with night-lights in the bay. Or perhaps the annual walk to the lighthouse on the top of Cap de Creus, during the local *festes*, to watch the sunrise. Or at least a Tramuntana-inspired sleepless night and a sudden flurry of poetic intent. But a quasi-military operation to block the motorway to France? Not in a million years.

We were sitting in the Maritim café having a beer and some delicious *patates braves*, enjoying the view and rubbing our calves after a steep climb up the Muntanya Negra when our son, Dylan, phoned and mentioned something about Pep, a motorway protest, the detention of the runaway president Puigdemont in Germany, and a free place in the car. I texted Pep. He told me to go into the Telegram app because the conversations there were encrypted. That was exciting enough. The plan was nitroglycerine drama.

I decided to go wearing my journalist's hat, but I was carrying a sepia photo of Bakunin close to my heart.

At 3.30am the next morning a heterogeneous group of people had gathered in the freezing dark by the roundabout at the entrance to the village. Apart from Pep and his wife Merçè, they were mostly pensioners in Lenin caps, and they were uncommunicative. I'm not sure whether this was due to the time of night, the sub-zero temperatures, my introduction to them as a journalist or their infamous *nos amb nos* character. I did discover that the murals and ever-expanding yellow ribbons around the village were mostly the handiwork of a zealous unemployed nationalist but generally, everyone was on collective mute. As a foreigner about to commit a crime in the name of their cause, I'd kind of expected them to share the coffee and cakes. To tell me their stories.

Good job I'd brought my own flask of tea.

At 4am we set off in a five-car convoy. No-one seemed quite sure where they were going except the guys in front. Thirty minutes later we pulled up in a car park in front of the biggest off-licence I've ever seen, The Wine Palace. If this diary entry were a WhatsApp message, I would put a laughing emoji right here.

By now there were scores of cars lining up to park, a procession of headlights snaking off into the dark.

We were directed down a muddy track through some fields around the back. I could hear the thunder of long-distance trucks rolling up the AP7 nearby but could see nothing except the muddy boots in front of me illuminated by the tiny torch from my mobile phone. Even that didn't last. Up ahead someone shouted, 'all lights out'. After that, I could only guess where the next puddle was by the swearing nearby.

We marched on. It was pitch black. It was icy. I had no idea where Pep and Merçè had gone. I was gripped.

61

After about ten minutes we came to a standstill next to a steep incline. It was clear from the noise we were close. It was intimidating. Everybody clambered up to the top to a find a wide-open area of scrub where, incredibly, somebody had previously, and purposefully, left hundreds of old car tyres. 'Strictly no lights, no mobiles. Everybody grab a tyre and await instructions.'

Somebody was on the phone, though. Otherwise, he wouldn't have known when to give the instructions. 'In five minutes we must be ready.'

I made my way to the front of the line and could now see the motorway below. The trees and bushes shook every time a lorry roared past. The first traces of light were seeping out from behind the Pyrenees in the distance.

Suddenly there was a shout. I could see three cars were slowing down on the motorway below creating an enormous slow-motion traffic jam until they suddenly stopped. '*Anem, rapid. va...* Go go go, now, quickly...'

Hundreds of people began to pour down the slope, rolling tyres over the ditch and through a bolt-cut hole in the fencing. I joined them, scrambling down with my tyre onto the tarmac. A barricade was erected with military precision. A small space at the edge was left for the three cars to slip off into the half-light of the empty motorway and then, the barrier was completely closed-up. A banner reading *Som Republica* was draped over the black rubber blockade.

Needless to say, if they were a '*Republica*' they wouldn't have had to get up at 3am and traipse through muddy fields to proclaim it.

The first vehicle in front of the barricade, surely a coincidence, was a huge Shell petrol tanker. I presumed that any intention they might have had of setting the tyres alight faded at exactly that moment. It's also possible that the lorry's presence explained why it took the police another six hours to work out what to do.

As the sun rose orange and magnificent over the snowy peak of Canigó and the plains of the Empordà, I watched people begin to dismantle the motorway sidings to construct new barricades. It was dramatic, but most probably futile.

I took some photos. I drank some tea from my flask. Had a crap in some nearby bushes. Came back and tried to crack some jokes, lighten up the atmosphere. But these boys and girls, boy, are they serious. I remembered that quote from Emma Goldman, 'If I can't dance it's not my revolution' and I thought, if I can't have a laugh then it's not my revolution. And then I thought, actually, it's not my revolution anyway.

The newspaper wasn't interested in the stuff I was sending them, and I didn't want to be around when the Cavalry arrived, so I went to look for Pep and Mercè. I found them sitting by a tree stump at the side of the motorway. She was looking cold and miserable, and her face lit up when I suggested leaving.

On the drive back to Cadaqués we stopped on a bridge over the deserted motorway so I could take a photo of that strange strip of emptiness stretching off into the horizon against the backdrop of the snow-capped Pyrenees. When I got back to the car, Pep was gazing out of the window.

'Fuck me,' he said, 'what a beautiful country this is.'

JC in prison pending trial, 172 days.

63

MARCH 27, 2018

Trying to get back home but the
traffic is terrible.   *10.04*

Clar, you blocked the roads, dafty.
                                        10.05

Bring me a croissant please   *10.06*

Imagine the mad bus driver in a
coach this morning...   *10.07*

Lua

Number 1 of 92 restaurants in Cadaqués

AlRivera
Lepe
👍 155

'Nationalist conflicts'

Customer: (Originally in Spanish) First thing I noticed was that the menu was only in Catalan, French and English which is perfectly fine (*obviously wasn't*, my initials) but what I don't understand is that there was no menu in Spanish, so I can't comment on the food because I didn't try it.

MANAGEMENT RESPONSE:

We are very sorry but the only language that does not appear on our menu, but we will include soon, is CATALAN. Since we opened, all our menus are in French, English, Italian and SPANISH, except for the names of the salads which are inspired by the names of Catalan winds. Still, it's a shame you didn't stay and try any of our food. You might have left in a better mood.

Date of visit: Oct 1, 2017

Keep on keeping on...the French

Cadaqués has always been a popular spot for any passing admiralty in the process of Mediterranean expansion. Its privileged position as a deep, relatively protected bay meant it was the perfect anchoring spot for anyone trying to cross the hazardous Gulf of Lion with its difficult currents and unruly winds.

The Greeks in 500BC. The Romans some three hundred years after in their search for Hannibal's elephants. The Visigoths working on what was later to become their *sangria* and sunshine holiday route. They all turned up at some point in their dinghies, with their buckets and spades, to build sandcastles on the village's pebbly shores. But it wasn't until the arrival of the French in the early Middle Ages that the place began to develop a serious identity crisis.

They just couldn't keep away.

Pretty much since 801 when King Lluís, the infant son of the French king and future emperor Carlemany, marched into Barcelona with his baby stroller, the animosity and battles that raged between the two countries that straddle the Pyrenees lasted a millennium.

A thousand years' worth of war that makes the Brits' 100-year war with the French look like a skirmish.

Things really kicked off in the early Middle Ages and by the end of the 16th century, there had been dozens of different wars.

Later, the French involvement in the Reapers' War (1640 to 1652) essentially put paid to any notions of a Catalan republic. Mainly because the Catalans asked for French help in their battle against Spain. They got it. Then France lost. Catalonia's fate was sealed in the subsequent Treaty of the Pyrenees in 1659. Essentially dismembered, it lost its northern territories to France: Spain ceded Roussillon as part of the deal between the two battling monarchies and established a frontier which remains to this day.

Did the treaty work? Like hell it did. The Frenchies were back in 1667, 1673,1678, 1680, 1689.

They came back for the Spanish War of Succession from 1701 to1714, which ended with the Treaty of Utrecht and the betrayal of Catalonia by the Brits, who until then had been fighting alongside the Catalans. The cash-strapped Brits were only too happy to find a way out of a financially draining war, and even happier to take possession of Menorca and Gibraltar as part of the deal. This treachery put paid to yet another Catalan push for independence. (The Catalans are nothing if not persistent.)

The attrition continued on and off for another century, culminating in the imposition of Josep Bonaparte (Napoleon's big brother) as the king of Spain. Known as *Pepe Botella* – Joey the bottle – due to his fondness for a tipple, the war that effectively ended his reign in 1813 was to be the last in this thousand-year conflict.

But why was it they kept on keeping on? Why all this continual bloody murder?

Maybe they just never got over what happened in 1285… in Cadaqués.

In the middle of one of these interminable wars, this time between the king of Aragon and Catalonia and French crusaders (Spain still didn't exist back then), the acclaimed

67

Catalan admiral Roger de Llúria (he was actually Sicilian) turned up in the Cap de Creus with six galleons and destroyed the boats of French navy. He also unexpectedly captured a galleon in the bay of Cadaqués which was carrying all the French navy's pay packets.

Not content with a simple victory, the following day he took the 300 injured of the surviving 600 French prisoners, tied them to the hull of one of the boats and sent them to drown at sea.

The remaining 300? He ripped out their eyes. Every last one. Roped them up and sent the lot of them, eyeless and bleeding, back to the French king in nearby Castelló d'Empúries. A loving missive.

At the sight of such barbarism, it is said the king lost his mind and never got out of bed again.

The French response has been long. And unforgiving.

These days they tend to arrive in Renaults and Peugeots instead of galleons. They use financial transactions instead of cannonballs.

In peak season, it feels like they own half of the village. They probably do.

'Rien n'est jamais fini…'

Emile Zola said that.

'I'm just mad about saffron
saffron's mad about me…'

Good Friday, March 30.

Crucifying

After the relative calm of the last few days, Cadaqués is now well and truly full of grockles, or *badocs,* as they call them here. The hardcore Easter weekend is upon us and to celebrate the arrival of all these click-happy visitors to this clickbait village, the locals (probably the same happy bunch I met in the early hours of Tuesday morning) decided to cover Port Doguer beach with small yellow crosses in remembrance of the political prisoners.

The effect was dramatic. Like a reimagining of the crucifixion scene from *Spartacus.* For hobbits.

And yes. It went viral. Click. Click. Click.

By 11am the photo had been taken hundreds of times, shared on WhatsApp, Facebook, Instagram, online news sites and probably even the Vatican Twitter feed. And there was me thinking the Catalan independence movement was strictly secular. That said, I wouldn't bet against the runaway President Puigdemont – currently holed-up in Brussels – being tempted to present himself up as some kind of Jesus figure (cue image of mop-topped Puigdemont embracing the Mannekin Pis and singing Depeche Mode's Personal Jesus, 'Reach out and touch faith').

As if the place wasn't crowded enough. Now we'll be getting the TV crews and independentologists. At the moment, however, the vast majority of this Easter influx come from across the border – the northern frontier that is. Not the imaginary southern border between Iberia and the virtual Catalan Republic.

The French seemed bemused by this quirky manifestation of Catalan religiosity and I wonder if they didn't just think it part of the typical Easter celebrations. But they were clearly keen to add it to their holiday photo gallery. Click. Click. Click.

It's a shame they aren't as bemused by the restaurants. Getting a table at any normal mealtime is worse than RyanAir boarding and most places don't do reservations. As a result, Monica and I have taken to always eating in the apartment to avoid the fights that break out in the queues, and the ones that sometimes erupt inside the restaurants too.

JC in prison pending trial, 175 days.

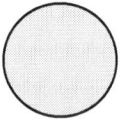

Tiramisu

Number 6 of 92 restaurants in Cadaqués

CatoFong
Cheam

👍 7

'Oh the French!'

We asked for the 16.50 menu. It was OK but for that price I really expected more quantity, I mean for the main course I only got one cuttlefish. But the worst was that the drinks weren't included, and when we went to pay, neither was the water. I really think for that price they could include the drinks. When I tried to complain, the owner, or whoever he was, just shouted at me in French (which I don't understand). It was really embarrassing. And even worse, bits of his spittle landed on my face while he was ranting. Yuk.

Date of visit: April, 2018

MANAGEMENT RESPONSE:

Bonjour,merci de votre visite, malheureusement, vous ne lisez pas les grandes ardoises dehors
et vous n écoutez pas ce que l on vous dit
Preuve: le menu de midi n est pas à 16,50€, mais 16,90€!!
Et nulle part il n est écrit ni dit que les boissons sont incluses !!
La seiche. ..vous connaissez le prix de la seiche ?? Vous savez que c'est plus cher que la daurade ????

71

Vous avez vu beaucoup de menu à moins de 20 euros avec de la seiche incluse ????
Vous voulez manger gratuit?
Vous ne lisez pas les panneaux. ..vous n écoutez pas ce que l on vous dit, vous ne savez pas le coût des choses , et vous vous permettez de juger et condamner...c'est lamentable.
Vous êtes un imbécile.

Jellyfish are:

Zombies.

Many jellyfish can clone themselves. If a jellyfish is cut in two, the pieces of the jellyfish can regenerate and create two new organisms.

Time travellers.

Some jellyfish are immortal. The *turritopsis dohrnil* is capable of returning to its embryo (polyp) stage in times of stress.

Eco-terrorists.

Jellyfish can shut down nuclear reactors. In the past few years, jellyfish swarms have been responsible for shutting down reactors in Sweden by clogging the intake pipes.

Cult musicians.

The *Phiialella zappai* jellyfish is named after 70s guitarist Frank Zappa.

Murderers

On average, jellyfish kill more people than sharks do.

A pain in the arse.

> The pebbles tremble and quiver
> the air buzzes with confusion.
> The enemy is at hand

April 28.

Stinging

The sea is a jellyfest. Not a drop of water, not one inch of shoreline, not a single cubic centilitre of shallow is free of this transparent goo.

While annoying, it's still not quite hot enough for it to be a complete disaster: sweltering on the beach in 80° heat and not being able to swim would be worse than queuing for restaurants.

When I first got to the Petit Llane this morning (one of the best beaches for an early dip), I'd been duped into thinking the pebbles were shimmering a welcome with the glisten of seawater and sunshine. It wasn't until I took off my sandals and squelched that I realized a whole universe of alien life was throbbing defiantly under my hopeful feet. So, I hunched up on the beach chair and watched them for an hour or so. There was a strangely transcendental pleasure to be had from watching those millions of tiny translucent hearts washed up and gently beating away their last moments.

Monica was fascinated and a long debate ensued about whether jellyfish actually have hearts. Google decided. They don't.

Unlike bees. Everybody's new favourite insects.

Back on our terrace, I found myself monitoring lines of them buzzing around lost and wondering what had happened to their house.

It was me… a couple of weeks ago, I'd spotted a steady trail of them going in and out of the hollow iron tubed structure that holds up the awning. While bees are great and all that, they are pretty annoying when you're trying to eat your lunch a metre away from their pied-à-terre in Cadaqués.

The simplest solution seemed to be just blocking the access holes with plasticine. Any doubts I might have had about their quasi-sacred nature and their hallowed hives, or the horror at this act of drone genocide, were assuaged by my claim to territorial justice. I mean, they do have all the countryside to themselves, and the bell tower looming above our apartment would make a perfect home. They might have hearts, but they don't have ears.

The plan seems to have worked. They buzz around the tubes for a while, banging their noses against the putty, before flying off disgruntled to somewhere else while I sit back and enjoy my land of milk and honey in the sunshine.

Monica is distraught, but more comfortable.

JC in prison pending trial, 203 days.

75

State-sponsored terrorism

It is sometimes surprising Cadaqués exists at all.

From as early as the 13th century the village suffered regular and brutal attacks from pirates, buccaneers, and privateers. Not only plundering the village for valuables but kidnapping anyone they thought might be worth a decent ransom.

Miguel Cervantes was picked up just in front of the bay on September 26th, 1575 and then spent five years imprisoned in Algiers before an order of Trinitarian monks finally came up with the gold. His captor was Dalí Mami.

In a typical piece of fictional hocus pocus, Salvador Dalí claimed to have been a direct descendant of this famous pirate. While the artist was almost definitely spinning a good tale (never say never), it is possible we do have the evil cut-throat Mami to thank for the greatest work Spanish literature ever produced. After all, five years is a long time to work on a plot.

It is difficult to pinpoint when all this freebooting started because in one notoriously brutal attack all previous records were destroyed.

On October 5th, 1543, 23 Turkish galleons lead by the famous Khair ed-Din – better known as Red Beard – entered Cadaqués and burned down the church with all the archives.

One story has it that Red Beard had been boasting about the 999 Christians he'd managed to scalp and was just waiting for his magic number 1000 (like Messi anticipating his 1000th goal against Deportivo de la Coruña). It was with this in mind he headed straight for the church. Here, to the horror of the petrified congregation, Red Beard ran up behind the priest as he raised the holy sacrament and chopped off his head with the cry: 'That is number 1000!'

There were dozens of further attacks and it wasn't until the 18th century that the villagers felt safe enough to start building outside the ramparts.

But why was piracy so rampant?

You guessed it. The French!

Half of these brigands were getting free access to the Catalan coast from the port of Marseilles thanks to King Francis I who used them to fight a proxy war against his neighbours.

In the Middle Ages, piracy functioned as a substitute for undeclared war.

Not unlike the American contractors G4S in the Middle East today.

Pirates, hey,

> I could reach up to that silvery sliver of a moon,
> waning crescent, like a cutlass
> and use it to cut out his silvery tongue…

May 11.

Adding. And subtracting

I arrived on my own again. Lately, I've been taking the early Friday bus. It makes the weekends longer and dinner is on the table for Monica when she arrives in the evening. It's a win-win, lucky life option.

Today, Pep and Mercè were waiting on the sun-drenched terrace of Casa Nun for lunch. It was a fake-friendly date. I owe him rent. They like company. I like to feel I'm living the life. We get on. Kind of.

She was quiet, clearly feeling miserable due to a bout of sciatica. He was effusive. He talked about helping him get his boat in the water and how fantastic Cadaqués was.

Now I think about it, every time I see Pep, he tells me how fantastic Cadaqués is, or the *pernil*, or the scenery, or the flat he's renting us… everything is always unbeatable. I had originally thought he was simply over-enthusiastic about life but after today I feel less generous. He's just another salesman.

We were talking the talk over salt cod fillets and fresh vegetables when, suddenly, he crapped in my wineglass. He was telling me about his latest megabuck project of 23 tourist apartments he was building in the coastal town of Badalona when he let slip, in the nicest kind of a way, that I had short-changed him a 1000 Euros in the last payment.

At first, I was merely surprised, then worried. Maybe I had misplaced the cash or made an error. But the doubts lasted as long as my one-sip *café solo*. I was sure, with the certainty of someone making an effort to live beyond his means, that I could not have made that kind of mistake. I just don't have that kind of cash floating about.

It was clear from the discussion that he obviously does.

It was upsetting. At the time I was all bravura and laughing but after the coffee and brownies, I was livid. This was somebody I have had political sex with.

I walked back to the apartment in a storm cloud despite the sunshine.

I don't know whether I was more wound up because it violently brought home the differences between our status or because it was an affront to my honesty. He was the rich guy with the house and the pool, and I was the tenant struggling with the rent (in his bijou holiday let) but under the illusion we were somehow on equal social terrain, maybe even friends. And that hurt. It was like being invited onto someone's yacht and then told to clean the toilets.

When I got back, I checked my bank statements, racked my brains and phoned Monica. I was right.

I texted him to confirm, and he apologized. But now it's out there. Floating, like a turd in the bay.

JC in prison pending trial, 216 days.

Casa Nun

Number 11 of 92 restaurants in Cadaqués

ChingShih
Tapei
👍 77

'Little gem'

So glad we tried this little gem. On the main drag by the water but set back enough to be more enjoyable. Sat upstairs by a window overlooking the cove at a table next to some people who looked very uncomfortable. One of them looked like a pirate, he had a big ring in his ear, and they were arguing. But even that didn't spoil the food. We had a good well-priced local red wine. Also loved the Zarzuela (baked seafood dish), rib steak with sliced potatoes and pepper sauce, and lastly, the rack of lamb with sliced potatoes. Everything was fresh, well-seasoned and delicious. A must try.

Date of visit: May, 2018

Eugeni and Lídia

Painters in Cadaqués might be as common as pebbles but philosophers are a rarer kind of rock.

One who did spend some time here, and leave his mark, was Eugeni d'Ors. His contribution to the Cadaqués pantheon? The mythologization of a lowly fishmonger: *La Lídia de Cadaqués*.

Calling himself Xenius (no false modesty in the onomatopoeia there for sure), d'Ors was a writer who claimed to elevate his weekly newspaper column to the status of a philosophical category. If a Kantian category is the appearance of any object in general before it has been experienced, maybe his myth-making was some kind of philosophical ruse.

Ruse or not, Lídia now has her own sculpture at the end of the Riba de Pitxot. Eugeni does not.

Lídia Noguer i Sabà, born around 1860, was the daughter of Sabana, the last witch of Cadaqués whose many powers included the ability to transform herself into a dog, control the weather and even travel at the speed of sound.

Not bad for the 19th century.

The night she died, Cadaqués was flooded with black cats.

Unfortunately for Lídia that kind of aura tends to get passed down. That her husband went crazy and hung himself and her two sons ended up in an asylum probably helped the narrative.

By the turn of the century, this possible witch-cum-fishmonger was running a celebrated boarding house and had gained a reputation for good food served up with a spectacular helping of aphorisms ('honey is sweeter than blood' being one of the most celebrated). Guests included Picasso, the architect

81

Puig i Cadafalch and, in 1904, the handsomely erudite Eugeni d'Ors.

It is said he was recovering from a bout of unrequited love. So... he was on the rebound.

During his stay, Lídia became a fervent admirer. An admiration that later turned into infatuation, obsession, neurosis, and ultimately... a bronze sculpture, several books, a bizarre headstone and a serenade by the composer Xavier Montsalvatge.

Surely the *suquet de peix* wasn't that good?

When d'Ors wrote his book *La Ben Plantada* in 1911, Lídia immediately identified with the main character Teresa – even claiming Teresa was, in fact, her name. She then began to interpret his subsequent newspaper articles as subliminal messages directed at her and began to bombard him with notes and messages. For 20 years. No reply.

It was at this point she told those who cared to listen that the village was divided into 'the good people' she could trust ('The Secret Society of Xènius'), and the 'bad people' (everybody else or 'The Society of Goats and Anarchists').

So how does pathological fandom for a little-known philosopher get you your own statue, a serenade and a couple of unofficial biographies?

Well, it helps if your neighbour is Salvador Dalí and he is not a goat or an anarchist. And the writer you have been pestering for decades decides the whole thing is worth a book deal.

In 1953, seven years after Lídia's death, Eugeni d'Ors returned to Cadaqués to gather information for a book about the woman whose million missives he had so consistently ignored.

And what do you know? Willy Wonka himself was a huge fan of Lídia. He loved the book idea and offered to do some illustrations.

It was Lídia's fishing cabin in Port Lligat that Dalí had bought in 1929 for himself and Gala (now home to the Dalí House-Museum) and it was Lídia who Dalí had described as 'possessing the most magnificent paranoiac brain, apart from my own, that I have ever come across'.

The book was on and Dalí was illustrating. Lídia effectively had her YouTuber and influencer.

In the epitaph of d'Ors book, *La verdadera historia de Lídia de Cadaqués*, it reads:

Rest here/If the Tramuntana lets you/Lídia Nogués de Costa/the Sibyl of Cadaqués/who magically and dialectically/was and wasn't/ *Teresa La Ben Plantada*/In your name/come together goats and anarchists/and the angels.

Eugeni d'Ors died in 1954, the same year the book was published. Spooky.

As for Lidia, due to the National Catholic moralizing of the time, it wasn't until 1989 that Dalí and his cohorts were finally allowed to get the headstone with d'Ors' intended inscription to her grave in the Agullana cemetery.

And guess what? Dalí died almost immediately afterwards. Spooky.

And there's the legend.

'You have to have a fine sensibility toward the ephemeral and the fleeting, and enough grace to eternalize it.'

— Eugeni d'Ors

83

No Larkin' Matter

This morning the young fathers are on parade.
One, a shock of hair, navy shorts, RayBan shades
 - very much the nascent Dylan '65 -
stands out to sea, his baby girl: sand and shells
golden curls. The tiniest of feet, mother of pearl.

They stand like statues face to face, still
not speaking, only the waves.
They stay like this in an infinite pause,
as if gauging the distance. Although, of course
they could just be playing, who blinks first.

Then, WHOOSH! Nifty at 60, Grandad crashes
into the picture with an inflatable unicorn thingy:
Aegaeon meets Jeff Koons, family fun and Loony Tunes.
Young dad seems to snap, out of it, slightly, hard to read
for his body language, is all at sea.

They then enthrone the itsy bitsy on her bouncy wouncy
unicorn dinghy, grandad says oh she's a cutey
but strange she hasn't uttered a single thingy
throughout this FUN, and as they wade off seaward
against the sun, it seems all three, are now struck dumb.

Before they reach the line of buoys, the fathers
look up left and raise their arms - backlit pre-war postcard poise -
to the woman in the high window on the whitewashed wall
crooked house, edge of the port. She waves back as mother
and daughter. And catches her breath, on the light in the water.

No Larkin' matter.

Busman's holiday

In Tripadvisor it says there are 92 restaurants in Cadaqués. Ninety-two is a huge number. A ridiculous number for a place smaller than Skelmanthorpe.

Once you take away the bakeries, takeaways, sandwich bars, the sushi bar, kebab shop and beach shacks there are probably around 60.

Of those 60, we have managed to eat in at least 40. Some of them many times.

That's kind of ridiculous too.

Of those 40, there might be a handful that stand out for one reason or another, but none glitter in the star-studded Michelin universe. In some cases, not for want of trying.

Compartir is a kind of Ferran Adrià derivation set up by three of his ex-students. They serve slightly over-priced, minimalistic and inventive concoctions which make phenomenal photographs on your Instagram feed. I was there a few years back. Can't remember what I ate. It was pretty. I'm glad Monica was paying.

At the other end of the scale in terms of style, and probably the most written-about restaurant in the village, is Casa Anita. In a cool dark space gouged out of the rock, it serves up simply cooked fresh seafood. No complications. High quality. No price list outside. Intimidating.

The owner Anita Mota came to the village over 60 years ago and earned her spurs dishing out stew to the local workers. She earned her reputation peeling Dalí's prawns. And she was well paid. Not just in cash. The steady stream of wannabes and semi-famous visitors following in Dalí's wake has given the restaurant much of its kudos.

In true *nos amb nos* tradition, her son Rafa Martin married into the village aristocracy when he exchanged vows with Carmen Faixó, whose family owned the Meliton café so often frequented by Duchamp and Dalí. They now head up a burgeoning empire which threatens to monopolize much of the town's offer. From Can Rafa to the Enoteca, from creperies to tapas bars, the MF initials are omnipresent.

To give them their due, they have also made huge efforts to recuperate the area's vineyards. Something they have successfully done with love and care. Respect.

Of the other 50 or so restaurants, none really sparkle but many are good. Most serve up a similar range of fresh seafood. Can Tito and El Grec are both worth a mention. Most of the places on the seafront offer similar lunchtime menus which usually consist of some combination of mussels, salad or gazpacho followed by fish of the day (invariably bream), grilled squid, or paella.

The arrivistes like Lua, Beirut and Mut push that global mishmash of modern beard-friendly fare: couscous, hummus or Japanese something. Coco has declared itself leader of the quinoa and carrot cake revolution while Talla has joined Compartir in the race for artistic innovation.

Generally, there is something for everyone and not much that will poison you. We have never eaten anywhere with photos of its food outside.

If you want to do as the locals do, and by locals I'm talking the second-homers, then you might find yourself in La Gritta on a Friday night or at the Chringuito de la Mei overlooking the Platja del Ros on a Sunday lunchtime.

And the ones who live here all year round?

For most of them, eating out is a busman's holiday.

> When a tongue asks for water,
> offer it salt.

May 20.

Seething

It's not often I feel like having a proper rant but last night rankled in a big way.

We have been going to La Gritta restaurant on and off on occasional visits but since we got the apartment, like most of the other second-home-locals, we now frequently call in on a Friday night.

Either driving up from Barcelona or catching the late bus (usually with the mad bus driver), there is never time to cook so it's a handy option. It's also the only place on the front that is always packed. The food is reliable, and I suspect there's an element of something I can only describe as 'fashionable tradition'.

This combination of popularity and reputation is strangely enhanced by the looming presence of the owner on the door. A mannish bespectacled woman with shoulder-length mousy brown hair, early 60s, always in a plain long-sleeved shirt, cigarette in hand. She scowls and hovers like a vaguely menacing maître d', doling out the dinner places at the doorway.

I have long suspected that her nod of recognition and the speed she gets you a table to be good markers of your place in the Cadaqués stratum. And let's face it, most people always want to be invited to the best parties, even if only to bitch about the guests. No matter who you are, or how high you fly, nobody ever gets over the schooldays' stigma of being chosen last in the football line-up.

But it's not just that. Whether it's Lower Manhattan chic or a fry-up in Grimsby, we all want that friendly acknowledgement, the 'all right mate, how's it going?' that makes us feel a little less lonely in this overpopulated, atomized world.

So, she snubbed us.

That mean-minded, stinky, smoking warthog snubbed us. Not even the slightest tilt of the head. No glassy-eyed good evening. Nada. Nix. Zilch. A true high-hat kiss-off and a cold muttered question: 'How many?'

To crown it all, when we got to the table, the waitress, who has seen me at least twenty times, asked if I wanted the menu in French.

La mare que la va parir.

JC in prison pending trial, 225 days.

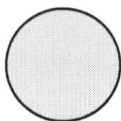

La Gritta (2)

Number 28 of 92 restaurants in Cadaqués

Finnegan
Dublin
👍 12

'On the job training'

We walked in and were met by a sulking rude teenager. It was early, about 7 pm, and there were two tables filled in the whole place. We asked for a table for two.
Shrug. Point. Can we have that table over there? No. So we walked out. It seems the wait staff does not like English speakers. And I'm not sure if the management is paying any attention.

Date of visit: May, 2018

MANAGEMENT RESPONSE:

We apologyze. We had talk, the same day that we saw this opinion, with waiter and we had changed his behavior. But this summer we have a lot of problem to find English speak staff. Next season we will find it for sure.
We wish that you will give us a new opportunity next day.

Isidre

Throughout the summer months, the bay of Cadaqués – one of the deepest natural ports in the region – resembles Henley regatta on steroids. Luxury catamarans, Russian private yachts and fancy skiffs crowd out the bathers and irritate local fishermen, but there is one boat that stands out like a vintage music box among mobile phones: the Sant Isidre.

Originally built in 1925 as a fishing vessel, it was requisitioned by the Second Republic Navy in 1931 after being caught used for smuggling. It has since been a warship, part of the Greenpeace fleet and a centre for scientific investigation, but fell into disrepair in the 1990s. Recently restored to its former glory, it is now used for tourist trips around Cap de Creus and night parties in the port. A thoroughbred stallion doing donkey rides on the beach.

Considered to be one of the 'historic' sailboats in Catalonia, its 600 square feet are a stunning example of the *vela latina*, the lateen sail. An innovation that changed the course of history. The maritime equivalent of the steering wheel.

Developed by the Arabs and then adopted in the Eastern Mediterranean, the lateen sail is a triangular sail set on a long yard mounted at an angle on the mast. It changed the course of history because up until then, the older square sails (like those used by Viking ships) would only let a ship be blown before the wind. So long as that wind did not vary much in direction the ship could raise the sail, but in variable winds or when navigating around complex shores it was either row or drift. Sink or swim.

The lateen sail meant that even wind blowing from the side could be used to propel the ship forward. No longer was a ship wholly at the mercy of the winds, and no longer was its range solely dependent on the ability of the crew to row.

That meant more space for cannonballs. More space for sugar. More space for soldiers. The addition of this innovational flag to the clippers also led to more exploration, more naval warfare, and a growth in international commerce. It meant Columbus going to America. It meant the British Empire, thank you very much. It meant the rise of the thalassocracy of which Catalonia and the Crown of Aragon was a prime example during the Middle-Ages.

And that means the beautiful Sant Isidre silhouetting out in the bay at sunset is not just another slinky little boat, but yet another signifier in the semiotics of Catalan symbology.

The round trip is 14.50 Euros.

> We slipped anchor at dusk
> sailing through a blizzard of bougainvillea.

May 21.

Boating

There was good fallout from the missing money mess. Due to what I like to think of as a nasty bout of capitalist guilt, Pep felt the need to calm the waters by handing over the keys to his garage and kayak. So, now, bike-parking and maritime endeavour are guaranteed for the rest of the year. And while this little plastic orange baby might not be the Sant Isidre, I am honoured to be an oar-carrying member of the ultra-exclusive Cadaqués boating community

It has certainly added some fun to the first weekend we have received non-family visitors.

Marc and Núria, who have been in ongoing separation therapy for the last five years, are here with their freckly, red-headed 10-year-old Maia. They still do most things together, sleep in the same bed, occasionally breastfeed, and seldom argue in public – and that's just Maia and Núria.

I was betting a morning on HMS Orange would tick everyone's boxes and provide a welcome distraction from marital strife.

In the end, Núria was overly worried about the safety of having Maia in a one-person kayak with another person but not on her own because she was too small and possibly not with Marc because she thought he probably wasn't responsible enough and then she did that smile to Marc which was really kind of asking him to be more considerate which he probably didn't see but Maia said she didn't want to go anyway so it didn't matter but then Marc tried to persuade her to join Dad in some fun and there was brief confusion on her face but she had picked up her mum's negative vibes and...

Marc and I took the kayak. The ladies walked. And talked. Like they like to.

We agreed to meet on the next beach and had a vague notion about getting to Pere Fet, which we eventually did. We even managed to get Maia on the kayak for a couple of hundred metres. It was a hairy ride though. Dodging the luxury motor boats and the speeding Zodiacs made me realize that Núria had probably been right to be wary. Fortunately, in the end, the outing was deemed a success and as the women strolled back to the apartment, I waited for Marc to bring the kayak back for the last stretch.

An hour later, I was still waiting. And the bay really isn't that big.

While I was waiting in the dwindling evening sunshine, I watched a garrulous group of women stroll past. As I watched them walk the talk and talk the walk, I felt a frisson. There was something fascinating about the way they moved together, the way they were speaking. The touch of an arm, a smile, a sudden laugh. This was what communication looks like.

I found myself wanting to close my eyes and walk with them. As though by closing my eyes I would somehow be able to float among them, invisible, and imbibe their magic.

Maybe I would have to visit the nearby islet of Mass d'Or where it is said that if you walk from tip to tip as the sun rises, you become a woman.

The legend doesn't mention what happens if you already are one.

Then... a sudden tap on my shoulder woke me from my reverie. Marc was back. He was looking happy. He had stopped off at the Casino for a quick beer.

One of the advantages of a kayak over the grander Fountain Pajot catamaran or Fleming motor cruiser is that you can pull it up on the beach if you fancy a swift half.

Three more of those and he'd be ready to walk the talk and talk the walk too.

Full steam ahead.

JC in prison pending trial, 224 days.

> Bright clouds settle along the rooftops.
> The scent of a light breeze softens the streets
> and from its cage, the bird marvels at the blue sky.

— Rosa Leveroni, poet, and neighbour of Dalí.

May 26.

Missing

Ever since I saw them last week, they are everywhere, these groups of women. The tiny beach in front of the Hotel Sol was full of them, splayed in starfish formation across the sand. Chatter chatter chatter. There was another crowd walking along the front in wide-brimmed straw hats and smiles, hen-party-goes-to-Ascot mode. Chatter chatter chatter. In front of the Casino at early doors, five or six twenty-somethings were standing laughing over bottled beers, hairful and happy. Chatter chatter chatter. On the beach in Port Doguer a small huddle of teenagers gathered tightly together around a totemic mobile phone. Chatter chatter chatter.

Chatter. All the time. Up close, snippets of conversation and words float in the air. Clouds of photons rise upwards in a kind of impressive semantic weather formation. Alto cumulus. Nimbostratus. Cirrus. Mahler's 3rd and Ricky Lee Jones.

On the rare occasions I catch a couple of men attempting something similar on a smaller scale, I can only see a cartoon speech bubble and random quarks inside a single ink-drawn cumulonimbus. Two-note chords on a Stratocaster.

96

I say on rare occasions because this weekend the men are missing. As if they had been kidnapped by pirates.

Monica said the two sexes were becoming 'separate more and more' but for the maths to add up that would mean seeing groups of men and women in equal numbers but apart.

In Cadaqués this weekend it's more a male lion in the female pride kind of ratio.

Eighty per cent of my gender have been vaporized.

Perhaps they're on strike in protest at the election of the first woman president of the *Societat l'Amistat* which runs the Casino. Originally women weren't even allowed in the bar.

There are no men on the beaches. There are very few on the bar terraces. They aren't shopping. None in the galleries. I can't see any looking for crabs or fishing off the Riba. There are no groups of boisterous boys jumping off the harbour wall at Pianc. There is no gym here and there is an international break in the football so they can't be somewhere watching that.

There are a handful of very old ones playing chess inside the Casino with the ghost of Duchamp but usually, at the weekend, the Casino is like a pub outside Old Trafford on match day.

Maybe the others are at home doing D.I.Y., setting up the awning on their terraces for that infernal summer I can smell just around the corner. Maybe they are out hunting boar among the holm oaks and tumbleweed up on the Serrat de les Malesses, or fishing for bream in Cala Culip. Maybe they are in their newly liberated kitchens, preparing dinner: *suquet de peix* and *taps de Cadaqués* soaked in brandy for dessert. Maybe they are all in Lloret de Mar on an enormous stag do, cocktail jugs in Disco Tropics.

97

Or maybe, they really have disappeared. Maybe, they just gave up.

This one? He's just sitting in his favourite spot on the terrace of the Bar Estic with a bottle of beer, watching the evening sun turn the sky pink. Sub rosa. Writing about their absence, which somehow, conjures up their presence.

Back home, on my terrace, the walls and tiles are full of microscopic red bugs which move around in tiny circles all day in the sunshine. I think they are clover mites. Clover mites reproduce parthenogenetically, no need for fertilization. They are only female.

Hold on, can you even have a defined gender if only one exists?

JC in prison pending trial, 229 days.

A single cupped flower of Bougainvillea
floats on the water, its carpel a tiny mast.
Magenta on aquamarine in the shimmer.

June 11.

Rowing, against the tide

Rain. And some extra days off work.

I had an argument with Monica about the safety of taking the kayak out in pre-storm conditions.

She's still cross even though I'm back safely.

Thunder rumbles behind the Pení like jungle drums.

Pathetic fallacy my dad says it is, this literary device which my fossilized error of a brain always gets mixed up with dramatic irony. I'm guessing that dramatic irony would be closer to me out on the kayak at the tip of the bay this morning, wrestling the Tramuntana and a growing swell, living out my adventurer fantasy just swimming distance from Catalonia's most affluent coastal resort. Meanwhile, somewhere nearby in the same sea, a boat full of hungry and thirsty North African immigrants turned away from negationist Italy heads in this direction.

Spain announced it would accept their arrival with *'brazos abiertos'*, open arms. The very same name of the boat carrying them.

This good-hearted, against the trend, politically risqué, and possibly suicidal move from Spain's new neo-social democratic PM (a surprise, following the loss of a confidence vote by the previous incumbent) means that any time now a monster

99

tanker packed with seething Islamic terrorists is about to crash into my good-natured left-wing kayak, leaving me paddling desperately against the vicious squalls of the right-wing intelligentsia. All the spectators know that disaster is imminent as the heavens open and the boats' paths are somehow intertwined. Cue dramatically engineered raindrops and The Inkspots crooning, 'Into this life some rain must fall, but too much too much is falling in my mine.'

Perhaps they will moor (sic) here in Cadaqués. Perhaps the local mayor will put them up in the hundreds of empty cinematic mansions and, on Sunday, organize a *paella popular* in the town square. Just in front of the huge mural worthy of Derry which reads *Libertat Presos Politics.*

It's hard to imagine anywhere further from Derry than Cadaqués.

Hizir bin Yakup, Jeireddin Barbarroja, Red Beard. Welcome back. It'll be a gas. Fake news. Fake news.

JC in prison pending trial, 244 days.

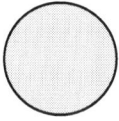

Mama Aicha

Number 29 of 92 restaurants in Cadaqués

Baldwin98
Boulogne
👍 11

'Flavourful'

After discovering this place, we went back as soon as we could, so we ate here twice in less than 12 hours. The couscous, tajine, salads and starters were fabulous. All the food is freshly home made in a one-woman kitchen. The hospitality and quality of food is something I've rarely seen in Europe. The food and the hospitable and humble atmosphere brought us right into the vibrant and flavourful world of Morocco. We will come again and would recommend everyone that likes home-made, flavourful and love-packed foods, to visit Mama Aicha. They don't sell alcohol, but you can take your own. They're Muslims. We drank the tea which was also authentic Moroccan style and amazing.

Date of visit: May, 2018

Obit

Firmo Ferrer was born in Cadaqués in 1921.

In 1939, at the age of 17, he and his family attempted to escape to exile. They had no choice: his dad had been the president of the local branch of the C.N.T. (the anarchist trade union).

As he explains in his book *Joventut Perduda* (Lost Youth), they managed to escape by getting a boat which had been forced to take refuge in Cadaqués, sheltering from the ferocity of the Tramuntana.

For once, it was a lucky wind.

Unfortunately, their luck didn't hold and over the next few years, he was imprisoned in various concentration camps in Rivesaltes and, later, a Nazi labour camp in Brest. When the war finished, Firmo stayed briefly in Barcelona before returning once again to Cadaqués in 1947 where he lived with his family for the rest of his life.

For forty years he ran a small grocery store with his wife in the village, but it wasn't until the 1980s that he found his calling and embraced his true passion: local history. He became a chronicler of Cadaqués. Perhaps *the* chronicler of Cadaqués.

Over the next ten years he wrote a dozen books which detailed the life, customs, geography, people, and even the proverbs of Cadaqués, including *Coses de Cadaqués (1986), Cadaqués des de l'Arxiu (1991), Topònims de Cadaqués (1999)* and *Contraban a Portlligat (1999)*. His work paints an intimate and honest picture of Cadaqués.

He was a contributor to the Cadaqués-based magazine *Sol Ixent*, and in 2010 became a founding member of the Centre for Cadaqués Studies, remaining its President until his death.

He leaves two children.

His funeral will be held this Friday, June 15th, 11am at the Santa Maria Church in Cadaqués.

Ferrer i Casadevall (Cadaqués, August 4th, 1921 – June 13th, 2018)

Up, on car park hill, along campsite road
by Dalí's bell, among olive grove,
lies a sleeping place, sighs a gentle breeze
soft as a shroud, a hint of the sea.

June 15.

Mourning

There was no way we were arriving in time for the funeral. Monica was working and, as usual, the Moventis timetable dictates our arrival. A shame, because I've enjoyed reading his stories about growing up and growing older in the village, and it would have been intriguing to see who turned out to see him off.

To be honest, it would have been fascinating just to take part in a Cadaqués funeral.

It was only on Wednesday when I saw a notice in the *Avui* newspaper that Firmo Ferrer had died and the funeral was today, this morning in fact. I suppose the traditional speed with which they organize Spanish funerals must be down to the heat in the era before refrigeration, and the habit stuck. It doesn't give you much time to sort out attendance though.

I hope I die with plenty of warning. So I can organize it properly.

Anyway, I thought the least I could do was pay my respects, so, in the light of late afternoon, Monica and I strolled up to the white-walled cemetery on top of the hill by Port Lligat.

He wasn't there. Or at least, we couldn't find any trace. No fresh flowers. No footsteps in the gravel.

Perhaps, with his anti-clerical beliefs, he'd been cremated.

We decided to stay and look around anyway.

When it was first built in the middle of the19th century, the setting must have been spectacular: next to the tiny sanctuary of Sant Balidiri, surrounded by olive groves with its arched windows offering views of the seascape around Cap de Creus.

Now, there's a scruffy bit of wasteland that serves as an overspill car park on one side, on the other, a gravelled campsite. The only olive grove remaining is on the slope between the cemetery and the sea, effectively Dalí's back garden. This means the cemetery vista imbued with meaning and solace (death, infinity of the sea, that kind of thing) now includes some oversized boiled eggs.

Monica was soon taking photos of a Josep Llimona sculpture to send to a friend of hers who is dating his grandson. I began to walk around among the columbarium, looking for names I thought I might recognize.

A columbarium is like a series of nesting boxes for the dead. Unsurprising, then, that it is also the word for a dovecote (there's a poem in there somewhere). The entrance to each niche measures about 3ft by 3ft. They are piled up five storeys high and are up to ten niches wide. That's about fifty people per block.

I don't think I'd fancy that really. Like going on holiday and ending up in one of those capsule hotels in Tokyo.

Clearly, the rich and powerful don't fancy it either. No niches for them. Most of the better-known village names lie in ornate family mausoleums. For the Raholas, Tremols and

Serinyanas no pantheon is too small, no ironwork too ornate, no marble statue too smooth.

Doric columns?

Here, have four.

Buckingham Palace opposite a Travelodge. All are equal in death.

Yeah, right.

At least everyone's got the same view.

After about twenty minutes of fruitlessly looking at names on niches (the only thing I'd determined was that inbreeding was the popular go-to marriage choice), I came across a corner full of foreigners. No niches here. Strictly in the ground with a tombstone for us, please.

They obviously didn't fancy the capsule hotel either.

I recognized the names of Captain John Peter Moore, Dalí's notorious secretary who got caught forging his master's signature, and Lanfranco Bombelli, the architect who'd designed some of the newer houses in Cadaqués. But Van Look, Quentin Henry Sackville. Mary Callery, Peter Harnden and his wife Princess Marie I Wassitchikoff from St Petersburg? Princess Wassitchikoff?? Who were these people?

So, I Googled them just now. Surprise. Most of the people in the corner of that foreign field were artists and architects. I was particularly annoyed with myself for never having heard of Mary Callery who was, apparently, a well-known American sculptor who had an architecturally noteworthy house in the village which was regularly visited by well-known figures from the 60s-70s art world.

The bodies in the ground were all artists and architects except for the Princess that is. She was a novel.

Marie was a Russian princess who escaped from the Bolsheviks and later ended up working in the UK Foreign Office in Berlin during the Third Reich. There, she was witness to a plot to kill Hitler, which she recorded in her book *The Berlin Diaries*. She wound up in Cadaqués after marrying the American air captain Peter Harnden who would later become designer, architect and partner to Bombelli here in Cadaqués.

And that's what I love. This place is so full of these stories, these artists, Russian princesses, trust-fund junkies and washed-up hippies. These funky outsiders are now so much a part of what the place has become. And yet, they're not. As their self-imposed separate lot in the cemetery suggests, they never breach the *nos amb nos* but settle instead for *nos amb ells, però no ben bé*: us with them, but not quite.

JC in prison pending trial, 248 days

Quiricus

The small recently restored Benedictine abbey of Sant Quirze de Colera is situated in a picture postcard valley in the Albera mountains, just a short drive from Cadaqués. Barring arguments over the accuracy of GPS instructions.

The abbey and its tiny chapel are surrounded by sloping fields with grazing cows. A brook runs alongside. Streams skitter down the hillsides. Beehives speckle meadows bursting with honeysuckle and rock jasmine. Larks and willow warblers dart across the sky. It looks like a painting from another era. The music is cowbells and running water. It is the essence of pastoral. Van Gogh's *San Remy*. Beethoven's *Sixth*. And there's a great restaurant which serves some amazing Perol sausage with baked apple.

Just don't sit with a view of the car park. Or think about the insides of the sausage.

There is a disturbing, if tenuous, parallel between the tasty sausage and the monastery.

Butifarra de perol amb poma is umami fantastic but is made from the tripe of small intestines, pig's head, heart and kidney. Deep down you suspect there may be a bit of testicle too. It's something about the texture.

The idyllic Sant Quirze de Colera is named after Saint Quiricus, one of the Martyrs of Tarsus. According to *Angels and Saints Online*, sometime towards the end of the first century, the three-year-old Quiricus was beaten to death while his mother was forced to watch. Her punishment for being a member of the notorious Fish on the Door Gang. Other versions claim that at the end of the third century, he was

108

simply thrown down the stairs for poking a Roman governor's nose. So, give or take a couple of hundred years – that's only Napoleon to Donald Trump – he was violently killed in the presence of his mother for somebody else's belief system.

He was only three. For God's sake.

Literally.

People now pray to him for family happiness.

His Saint's Day is June 16th.

Both the monastery and the sausage hide nasty secrets.

June 16, 2018

I rented a really cool car *17.05*

No mad bus driver. Yeyyyy *17.05*

So now we can take your papis to that spot near Garriguella... *17.07*

> As the equinox approaches, the satellites in geostationary orbit
> find it difficult to maintain power. This phenomenon,
> which affects most modern navigational systems,
> is particularly notable in zones of telluric influence.

June 17.

Driving

My mum and dad have been staying in the apartment for the last couple of weeks; finally, someone is taking advantage of the place other than us.

I have been constantly amazed how few of our friends ask to borrow the apartment. Perhaps we have too few friends. Perhaps they don't feel comfortable 'borrowing'. Perhaps they love us so much that they only want to be here when we are. In that case, we have four and a half friends so far this year.

Anyway, my folks being here means that other than staying up on the terrace and arguing about politics – cue disillusioned, ex-communist, ex-classicist bemoaning his lack of ability to see anything in the new 'new left' and decrying the evils of nationalism versus contentiously rabid son who, as John Cleese said, paid five pounds for this argument… mum weeping into wine, 'oh please stop arguing'… wife looking at me admiringly (I think…), she does like to see a bit of political fire in my blood) – we feel obliged to make an effort and take them places. So, we rented a car.

I am embarrassed about just how clichéd our car trip arguments have become. Before GPS I was always a terrible co-pilot. Now I am a terrible co-pilot who has two people to argue with. And this happens frequently in front of my parents. I can feel them looking at each other knowingly in the backseat. Probably grinning at each other like kids.

You would be amazed how easy it is to get lost. Even when you are coming from and going to a place which has one road in and one road out. Such are my navigational skills.

Today we drove up to the nearby monastery of Sant Quirze which Pep had pointed out to me on the drive back from the motorway blockade. 'Oh, there's a lovely little-known spot just over there,' he said, signalling some bare-looking hills.

Just over there.

Rabos is the nearest village to the monastery. It is tiny. We drove around its four houses, four times, before I let Monica choose the way. This was after having previously arrived at the French border in search of Baron Munchhausen's castle, which we never found.

- Where is it we're going exactly?

- I don't know, I just thought it would be nice to visit that castle we went to that time before. Make a day of it.

- Well, we've gone past it. It was miles back.

- How am I supposed to remember the exact way?

- But you put the wrong address in the GPS.

- But GPSs don't know everything. You've driven there before. You should know.

- I think I recognize this road. Didn't we drive along here a moment ago?

- Where exactly are we going?

- Don't ask me.

Sigh. Growl.

- Shall we all just stop here for a coffee and clear our heads?

111

Sant Quirze was beautiful though. Pep was right. And once I'd stormed off up a beaten track to let off some steam, we had a fabulous lunch in El Corral before driving back to Cadaqués to the sounds of Keith Jarret's Koln concert. Happy just to know the way. And in time for an evening swim.

It's been a lovely day and now I am back on the terrace drinking in the sunset. And drinking. In the sunset. Preparing for tonight's round of Dionysus dialectics.

JC in prison pending trial, 250 days.

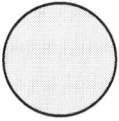

El Corral

Number 1 of restaurants in Sant Quirze

DocHolliday
  RHBYorks   **'Well done guys!'**
👍 14

Cooking here is mostly grilled meat. Vegetables are heavy on beans and chips. Portions are good, wines are good value. Very nice apple sauce and sausage for starters but nothing to write home about, you might think. But what gets this place a high rating from us is its location miles from the nearest tarmacked road, in a beautiful valley, next to a medieval monastery. We walked down to it from the Col de Banyuls, taking around 90 minutes. You can drive too from the south, right up to the restaurant with no problems in a normal car, if you take it gently on the bumpy roads and don't get into arguments with your GPS.

I can't get over the courage it must have taken to start a business like this in the middle of nowhere.

Well done guys!

Maybe this review will help put you on the map.

Date of visit: June, 2018

Joan

Another Saint. This time, one with a Superbowl-size reputation.

The Saint's day of John the Baptist, Sant Joan, is a huge holiday in Catalonia. And the night before, possibly its biggest party. Yet, unlike Christmas, almost no one ever spares a thought for who it is they are supposed to be celebrating. Probably because it's not really about him.

The *revetlla de Sant Joan* (the eve of Saint John) is essentially a riotous pagan party on the shortest night of the year. An ancient celebration involving fire, cakes and dancing. You might think the fact it misses the solstice itself by 48 hours is just an extreme example of the Iberian attitude towards punctuality but it is actually the Catholic church, yet again, wresting control of a popular bit of debauchery from the people and moving it to the nearest Saint's day to give it the veneer of respectability.

The pagan tradition is why the party is still associated with witchery and superstition. In Organya, in the Catalan Pyrenees, passing babies over the flames remains popular. It is also said to be a good night to burn your wishes on scraps of paper in the hope they come true, and a bad night to look in the mirror (which makes sense if you are seriously partying).

Mostly though, these days, it means a very late dinner followed by a special cake with toasted pine nuts (*coca de Sant Joan*) and cava before bonfires, fireworks and – if possible – a swim in the sea at sunrise.

Burning effigies of your enemy is a relatively new development.

> There's nothing worse than people
> who dress friendly, and act snooty.

June 22.

Madding

So, I'm in Bar Mut for a change. A nice play on words; *mut* being dumb in Catalan, while phonetically Bar Mut sounds like *vermut*, as in vermouth. It's a shame the waiting-staff live up to the literal meaning. Not even a nod. After all this time.

I don't feel much like writing really. But being a man of habit, I wanted to get an early-doors and escape the relatives. Writing is the excuse.

This weekend it's Conxita (Monica's mum) and Joan (confusingly, Monica's bother). 'Confusingly' because despite having lived here for 25 years, the Anglo-Saxon in me still has trouble not thinking of Joan as a girl's name when in fact it's the Catalan of Juan, as in Don Juan, the famous Mediterranean Lothario.

June is obviously the month of choice for family. Between my folks and hers, the apartment will have been full almost every day. Warm days, long summer evenings and not too many people.

Sitting here watching all the cars pulling into Port Doguer, I can see that last point is about to change.

Tomorrow is my favourite night, in my favourite place. And it's clear a lot of other people feel the same way.

The eve of Sant Joan in Cadaqués, *la revetlla*. Bonfires, fireworks, music and madness, or *rauxa* as they call it around here.

Catalans have long self-identified as having two character traits: *rauxa* and *seny*. *Rauxa* is a kind of wild madness you would never suspect when watching their national dance of *sardanes* (to *rauxa* as Stalin is to laissez-faire) but could probably guess at when you see them parading down the street wearing giant papier maché heads. Or organizing an illegal referendum to secede from Spain and expecting acquiescence.

After all, Spain is the country that invented the Inquisition.

Seny is the other side of the coin: a mixture of common sense and pragmatism which gives Catalans an uncanny knack for business and a sense of planning which has marked their enormous pro-independence rallies.

Over the last few years, it has been the norm for over a million people to pre-buy that particular year's colour T-shirt and congregate peacefully at exactly 17.14pm on September 11th to perform a short and carefully prepared choreography. It is a Guinness world record photo shoot.

Although, that too, is somehow a kind of madness.

The date and time of these huge demonstrations represent Catalonia's most famous defeat at the hands of the Spanish in 1714: the end of the Spanish War of Succession, and pretty much the end of Catalonia's hopes of becoming an independent state.

I have ordered a sack full of sky lanterns from Amazon so I can join in tomorrow's collective lunacy. Just hope this wind dies down. Or at least changes direction.

116

Otherwise, there is going to be a forest fire of epic proportions.

JC in prison pending trial, 255 days.

A poster on the local noticeboard:

Revetlla de Sant Joan a Cadaqués, 2018.

A les 20h al Passeig: arribada de la Flama del Canigó
(the arrival of the flame from Canigó Mountain)

A les 20:30h al Passeig: Sardanes amb la Cobla els Rossinyolets
(folk-dancing in the square with the Little Mushroom Orchestra)

A les 23h Portell de sa Riera: 'Foc de Sant Joan'
(bonfire on the beach in front of the casino)

A les 00h en el Passeig: Festa de Sant Joan amb Muntband+DJ PD Ivanote.
Barra a benefici de UE Cadaqués
(party in the square with Up Band and DJ Little Ivan. All bar proceeds to Cadaqués FC)

A photocopy taped to a tree by the beach:

**Cremem la monarquía
Encenem la Republica!**

**Burn the monarchy
Light up the republic!**

The beach is littered with the spent carcasses of fireworks,
the smell of cordite lingers in the air.

June 24.

Aching

I woke up feeling ragged, peeled my eyes open and looked at my phone only to discover that Cadaqués was all over the national news. Again.

How had I missed that? Too much *rauxa* for sure.

It seems that during last night's celebrations, the whole village had collectively burnt images of the Spanish King, a heap of Spanish politicians and Judge Pablo Llarena, the man held responsible for the incarceration of the Catalan leaders. This probably happened all over Catalonia but Cadaqués being the trendy media watering hole it is means the lazy hacks got their byline without having to leave the party.

At the time I must have been on the other beach with Joan and another fifty intoxicated pyromaniacs.

Trying to ignite the Chinese sky lanterns was an exercise in futility: cheap defective Amazon shit, clumsy drunken European men, and a Levant wind. The paper kept catching fire before the ballon was full of hot air. The only one (from a dozen) we managed to light, soared off in the wrong direction, zooming up over the church towards the woodland kindling instead of floating softly out and over the bay, disappearing gently into an atlas of stars.

Monica was standing on the quayside, with a bemused Conxita, shouting at us to stop. Yelling about fire hazards, stupidity, wind and alcohol. She was right of course, but the little fire devil had his claws well and truly buried into us by then. What's more, we were surrounded by a group of gushing drunken Japanese girls egging us on. 'Are you creatives? Are you creatives? Only creatives would do this...'

I don't really know what 'a creative' is, but 'a practical' would definitely have bought a family pack of fireworks from Tesco.

Later, after gazing into the embers of the bonfire on the beach in front of the Casino (the one where those worse-than-paedophile-inexorable-Catalan-*independentistes* must have committed those treasonable offences), I managed to get in my obligatory midnight swim. I floated happily in the dark water, watching the fireworks light up the sky and feeling the bass from the mobile disco like a depth charge. And thankfully, when I swam back to shore, I wasn't met by a wall of blokes with their dicks out emptying their bladders into the sea. That had really ruined the whole experience last year.

This year it was just Monica, waiting with a towel, telling me it was time for bed. Conxita and Joan had left ages before. 'You've got that look on you, you know the one.'

Oh, that look. It caused a few sparks of its own back in the day, that look. Sparks of the wrong kind.

But she was right, again.

Sugar on my tongue.

JC in prison pending trial, 257 days.

Summer

> Being set on the idea of getting to Atlantis
> we sailed direct with the Cadaqués divers.
> When we arrived at the spot,
> an inflatable mermaid with only one eye,
> and around her neck a terrible sign,
> '*Tancat per defunció*':
> Closed owing to bereavement.

June 30.

Diving

Unbelievably, today I had my first pre-breakfast dip in Doggy – as my Dad recently renamed our little beach. And what a swim. What a dive. What a snorkel.

I got there before the oldies had set up their Maginot Line of foldable beach chairs to outflank the mother and baby offensive.

So, I was early.

Early as in first.

Except for some guy who must have fallen asleep on the way home from the bar. But that doesn't count. Technically, he was last.

Knowing the water at this time is always crystalline, I took my old-style snorkelling kit. I say old-style because the height of this year's snorkelling fashion is a one-piece breathing tube and a GoPro. This new contraption looks like a cross between a gas mask and an astronaut's helmet.

State of the art or not, I'm betting these scuba fashionistas haven't seen Guy Cooper from Hawaii on YouTube claiming the mask was to blame for his 'water-bug' wife's death, or the *CBS This Morning* headline: 'Spike in deaths raises concerns over full-face masks.'

A dangerous increase in carbon dioxide intake, they said.

I check these things.

Sometimes, I'm careful.

Unfortunately for endangered marine life, other times I'm not.

I swam out to investigate the huge forests of seagrass that are so common around here.

These Posidonia meadows are a good indicator that the water is clean as they tend to die off at the slightest hint of pollution: a good thing to know if your old-style snorkelling kit means a seawater smoothie is your go-to breakfast choice.

Then, about 200 yards from shore, hiding deep among the swaying fronds, I saw it. The biggest mussel ever. The length of my arm. The dinosaur egg of bivalve molluscs.

That baby was coming home with me.

Ears popping, I swam down to pick it up. It was stuck fast. I had to come back up for air before attempting another dive. At that point, I should have guessed this was no ordinary over-sized piece of shellfish. But by then I was in full Jacques Cousteau meets Rambo mode. A destroyer of worlds.

The second time down, I managed to loosen it up, but it was still resisting trophydom. In the end it took four dives for me to yank it off the seabed.

I swam excitedly back to the beach where I ripped off the annoying ugly hairy stuff that had been tying it down (another big error). Encrusted with barnacles and dried seaweed, the shell was slightly open. The inside gleamed. It was a small cave of mother-of-pearl, bathed in orange-gold. It was a priceless treasure from Atlantis. It was this month's rent.

The old ladies, the mothers and the children, who had by then arrived on the beach, were all staring at me intently as I came out of the water.

Were they awestruck or did they already know what I was about to find out?

I rushed back to the flat and immediately Googled 'giant mussel shell' (3,730,000 results, 0.44 seconds). It was a fan mussel. A pen shell. Pinna Nobilis. A sea-wing.

An endangered species.

A mass mortality event.

S.O.S Pina Nobilis.

Oh, the shame!

In less than five minutes I discovered that it was in danger of extinction. It was protected by a 58-page EU directive. It was not to be touched. There was an email address to be reached in case of sightings. And the ugly hairy stuff I'd chucked away? Priceless sea silk, the golden thread of Jason's fleece.

I had broken the law and I couldn't even make a profit from my treachery.

What kind of a man was I?

Now I'm sitting here writing about it, looking out over the bay of these magical invisible forests. I'm feeling guilt, thinking justification.

I mean, how was I supposed to know?

They could have put a sign.

It turns out this rare form of sealife, almost unique to the area, is a mass mortality event happening right now, here in snorkelling heaven.

And they can't even manage a sign warning off ignorant predators?

Then again, they don't even have a sign asking people not to leave their fag ends on the beach. People probably already know that though. If they stopped to think about it, it would be obvious.

If they stopped to think, it would be obvious.

Nobody wants to lie down half-naked in an ashtray.

Or swim in a lifeless pillaged sea.

People.

What are we like?

JC in prison pending trial, 263 days.

Diving for Pearls
Submarines, Greeks, and Gin and Tonic

Less celebrated but equally as important to village life and with its own cast of heroes and villains, diving has always been an integral part of life, and death, in Cadaqués.

These days, diving around the Cap de Creus is a big tourist draw. Several companies run huge operations taking people out to visit the vast underwater canyons. It is a popular but risky pastime. It is not unheard of to see a yellow rescue helicopter land in Port Doguer to pick up the body of some diver who has suffered a fatal decompression.

It was here, between 1855 and 1857, Narcís Monturiol invented the submarine. The utopian communist was on the run from yet another clampdown by an authoritarian Spanish government when he saw the village's coral divers risking their necks and came up with an ingenious plan to make their lives easier. And, hopefully, make himself a buck or two in the process.

The coral is known as red gold. The Greeks said it came from the blood of Medusa's head following her decapitation. And at up to 1,000 Euros a kilo, its value inevitably encourages illicit behaviour. As a result, even though diving for coral around Cap de Creus is now strictly limited, and in most places illegal, it hasn't stopped the pillage.

Pirates and smugglers.

Old habits die hard.

Most of the villagers won't mention these few remaining coral pirates for fear of reprisals. They are usually well known and well off, and nobody has forgotten the night of 1998 when they set alight the house of a rural protection agent and killed his dog.

One local rural protection agent, who we can call Jordi (not his real name), said: 'It saddens me, there's almost nothing left. These are people we know who do this, like Josep Maria Lloveras. He's been taking the stuff for over 20 years. But he's powerful. He's got a hotel and apartments... He's been sanctioned various times by the state authorities but he has great lawyers and he just gets away with it...'

Red coral grows so slowly that every time a diver takes a piece it's as if he were ripping up a centenary oak tree on land.

A shame Mr Lloveras didn't die from a decompression.

The most legendary group of divers in these waters were a team of Greeks called on to work on the salvage operation of British steamer the Llanishen, which sank off the coast in 1917.

From Simi in the Dodecanese islands, they were famed for their diving skills. On Simi, tradition prevented young men from marrying until they had managed to get a sponge from at least 20 fathoms deep.

After the Llanishen salvage operation, the group decided to stay. They felt at home. Cadaqués looks like a Greek island and there was plenty of work. Including diving for that prized coral, which in those days was still a legally depletable resource. Sponges, too, were hugely profitable and still legally depletable.

When the Spanish civil war broke out in '36 and the locals decided to start depleting themselves instead of the sea life, most of the divers returned to Greece. Except for Kostas Kontos. He married local girl Maria Batllori.

Their grandchildren don't dive. But they do form part of the village's permaculture.

Constantí runs a small restaurant on Carrer Unió called Es Grec while Manel recently won the Mediterranean Inspirations cocktail festival.

The name of his creation? The Gin-tonic Kontos. It's on sale at the Bar Boia on the beach. If you get the right waiter.

Cheers.

July 8, 2018

Dylan, have you got the loopy driver?
19.10

Don't know. Looks normal to me.
19.12

Skinny, balding. Talks to himself.
19.13

Nah. He's short, dark and quiet.
Looks a bit Greek
19.14

What is it – this marvellous thing
that lasts only a moment, but touches the soul
at the fading of light with warm marigold?
'Just a tiny star falling down,' she laughs,
the ice cubes tinkling at the bottom of her glass.

July 9.

Becoming

Our youngest, Dylan, and his girlfriend, Laura, are here for the weekend and there have been some glistening moments. The ones where you feel the descendants' transcendence loop in full force. The ones that make up for all the arguments about dirty dishes and shoes in the hall.

The meaning of life is probably hovering somewhere around the table when you are having a drink in the soft evening glow of a beautiful bay with your 19-year-old son, his girlfriend, and your gorgeous wife. When the sea is glimmering with irridescent pink gold. When the conversations are warm and hopeful. When the gin and tonics are aromatic and fresh.

Oh, those gin tonics! The lovely Gaia at Bar Estic has recently acquired a Gin Trolley, complete with spices and innumerable unfathomable choices of Mother's ruin. An irresistible triple incantation.

Gaia is a chatty, tattooed, blonde twenty-something (works in summer, travels in winter), the daughter of a true pirate-fighting *Cadaquesenc*. Her grandad used to go out in his rowboat with a rifle and shoot bits off the luxury yachts for fun.

129

So last night, there we were. On my favourite terrace with the best evening views, the friendliest waitress, feeling the love, and sipping: Millers with coriander (me). Brecon with cinnamon (Monica). Tanqueray and Aquarius (Dylan). Mare with rosemary and essence of smoke (Laura). Personality choices every one.

It was at some point when we were all tasting each other's drinks – essence of smoke, huge error – when I heard a voice in the back of my head saying something about that old adage of becoming your father. He loves his gin, and I've been in this same loop with him. Although never drinking Aquarius. Genetics isn't as exact a science as you'd think.

At first, I wasn't sure about the arrival of this thought. Was it taking the shine off the emotional fireworks? It's not that I fear becoming my Dad, although I'd happily skip the getting up at dawn part, I just hate it when cliché invades my metaphysical magic.

Then I realized that the thought just added to the general ambience in the Pensieve. By thinking of him, I had brought him to the table too. Larios in hand, having a gin-tonic with his son's son.

Expecto Patronum.

My Dad studied classics.

I read Harry Potter.

JC in prison pending trial, 272 days.

Es Grec

Number 9 of 92 restaurants in Cadaqués

JCosteau
Fontaine   **'Authentic'**

👍 71

Fantastic seafood off the beaten track on a cobbled street. We had the plankton rice and some razor clams. Both delicious.

But the best thing...all the photos of the old divers on the walls. You must get the owner to tell you all the stories about his grandad and the divers and to show you all the model boats he makes.

He's a true artist. A lovely an unforgettable lunch. Thank you Es Grec.

Date of visit: June, 2016

Shopkeepers

For a place with a population no bigger than Eccleshall in Staffordshire, Cadaqués has a surprising number of food stores, supermarkets, bars and cafes. Probably because at the height of summer, the population increases ten-fold. And like a perfect microcosm of the outside world, a few of the village shopkeepers have managed to emulate the worst aspects of the multinationals' voracious practices.

There may be no Walmart or Starbucks, but MF (for Martin Faixo) and Es Fornet are doing their utmost to establish mini-empires and squeeze out the competition.

The MF trademark is especially guilty of crimes against diversity. Sometimes when I see the plaque MF by the door, I think it's MF for mafia.

Operating from its laudable vineyard base at the top of the hill, the dynasty includes Can Rafa, Casa Anita, Enoteca MF and Versatil. The last two being particularly irritating examples of over-priced, puffed-up tapas joints. Shameful little exercises in self-aggrandizement.

Es Fornet, as its name implies, started out as a pleasant bakery/cafe in the village square. It now boasts the Es Fornet Rotisserie, Es Fornet Sushi and Wine, and the Es Fornet yoghurt ice cream parlour. The Es Fornet vegan pizzeria will surely be next.

There are also three big-chain supermarkets which offer fresh produce, including fresh fish stalls and their own bakeries.

Even more worthy then that the smaller establishments survive.

There is a good little eco-grocer's tucked away in an alleyway off the main street and another quirky grocer's in a garage opposite the Condis. Serraplà in the old town is a locally sourced butcher, and there is still a proper old-time ironmonger's despite the presence of a cheap-as-chips, Chinese-run, sell-everything shop up the road.

There are two specialist patisseries and the Forn Sanés on the seafront sells wholesome artisan bread. Their spelt loaves are particularly tasty.

But you need to pre-order them.

And get there early enough to make sure they don't sell yours to a true blood – or a *pota negra* as they call them around here.

Nos amb nos, remember.

> Give us this day our daily bread
> and forgive us our trespasses
> as we forgive them that trespass against us.
> We can always buy it somewhere else.

July 26.

Drifting

I think it's July 26th. I'm not sure. We are now five days into what is going to be the long summer haul. No more weekend breaks.

Look at that: 'The long summer haul', 'no weekend breaks'. It sounds like hard work, like I'm almost complaining. But this is proper holiday mode, where lazy days drift by without numbers. Where the only choices I have to make are: which beach? Which bar? Sunshine or shade? Sleep or swim? Effusive hello or subtle nod and eyes down mumble?

It's been six months since we started coming, and to be honest, I'd expected a bit more community spirit. A bit more *bon dia, com va, fins demà, ix!* I'm not asking for a hug every time I order a beer but it would be nice if when I left my name down for an order in the baker's they didn't act like they'd never seen me before.

Lately, we have taken to ordering a spelt loaf at Forn Sanés. We had first come across it at a lunch at Pep's place a while ago (in the days before I became a conniving tenant and he became a rapacious landlord and we still got invited to lunch). A firm white cob with a good crust, equally suited to being rubbed with tomatoes, drizzled with olive oil and layered with cured ham as to being smothered in butter and jam.

This morning was the third time I have been to this baker's to collect my pre-ordered bread and they have denied all knowledge of me and my loaf.

There can't be many English men who regularly go in there to place an order.

Maybe that's the issue. Maybe she doesn't like tourists. Maybe she doesn't like anyone.

I don't think I'd like anyone if I had to get up at 4am to bake them bread.

Maybe she should change her job.

Either way, taciturn is a compliment.

- Good Morning.

- Is it?

- Hi, yes, I ordered a white spelt loaf yesterday.

- Name?

- I'm Ryan.

- No.

- What do you mean no? I am, and I definitely ordered it.

- No.

Sigh (hopeful but pessimistic).

- Well, never mind, have you got one any anyway?

- No. You have to pre-order.

I did, I always pre-order.

- This isn't right. This has happened loads of times. I come in here and you say I haven't ordered the bread. You don't even have my name.

- Don't know about that.

135

- It's true. Maybe you should ask the woman who was here last night.

- I might have sold it.

- Ah, so you did have my loaf. So why did you sell it to someone else?

- You should get here earlier.

- It's 9 o'fucking clock.

Us with us, hey.

No point in going to an ironmonger's and hoping for a sugary bun.

JC in prison pending trial, 289 days.

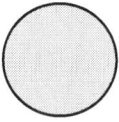

MF Enoteca

Number 18 of 92 restaurants in Cadaqués

BobParker
Bordeaux **'Trying'**

👍 1412

I had very high hopes for this place given all the reviews. The tapas were extremely average and often had some critical flaw (potato omelette was tasteless, missing salt). The lovely octopus was sitting in some kind of glue-flavored sauce and they brought us the wrong seafood we had ordered.
Of note, the local vineyard that owns the place is really trying hard with their wines but they are all a bit aggressively flavoured and not exactly easily drinkable.
I might have forgiven all of these things if the price wasn't towards the high end of the price range. We spent 70 Euro for two people with minimal alcohol and ended up leaving hungry. The best things were the crepes which were both filling and cheap.

Date of visit: July, 2018

The squatting dog

Originally built in the 13th century and set atop the stronghold that is the old town, the Santa Maria church has two historical claims to fame. Both involve pirates and arson.

The first attack in 1444 wiped out most of the town records. An event which has allowed local historians a margin of poetic license ever since, and also led to the building of a wall to protect the area.

The second attack in 1543, led by Red Beard himself, made light work of the wall. So complete was the destruction it took another fifty years to rebuild both church and wall. This time the job was paid for by the *penes* from the local fishermen: money gained by working on public holidays and weekends. This act of altruism and good faith, which had nothing at all to do with the fact that the Spanish Inquisition was in full swing at the time, is celebrated in a poem by local writer Frederic Rahola:

L'església del meu poble
la feren els pescadors
treballant els jorns de festa
en bé del nostre Senyor.

It translates literally as:

The church in my town
was made by fishermen
working on public holidays
for our Lord.

138

But with the rhyme added back in would probably look like this:

> The church in my town
> was built by fisherfolk
> working at Christmas
> was some kind of joke.

Aside from its Heavy Metal history, the church also boasts one of the oldest organs in Catalonia (1690) and with a flamboyance worthy of Dalí himself, one of its most spectacularly camp altars. No mean feat. Because altars, in Catholic churches, are probably the campest thing going in ecclesiastical interior décor.

And this is high camp. The Freddie Mercury of altars.

Celebrated in a collage by Richard Hamilton who pre-photoshopped a big band into the foreground, the baroque altar of gilded wood (1729) has a sea-faring theme – the least the fishermen deserved after all their contributions.

The price paid to Pau Costa for the job is hard to calculate but at the time it was 4500 *lliures*. If we take a *lliura* at the time having the value of 327 grams of silver, at today's prices that's a cool half a million. Damien Hirst prices.

The immense golden meringue is peopled with cherubs, saints, and the heads of fishermen and sailors whose faces poke out of the woodwork like Captain Cat's dead dears. But pride of place goes to a huge shiny Burt Reynolds lookalike attached to one of the main pillars.

Muscles bulging, wearing a skin-tight red vest, skinny blue shorts and a gold sash, one hand on his hip, the other raised in a wave, he seems to be saying: 'Come on up boys. I'm dead.'

In the early days of the civil war in 1937, a member of the local anarchist militia chopped off this waving hand. Said it looked like a fascist salute.

It was restored after the war. The winners obviously had no problem with that particular salute.

And the squatting dog?

Well, if you are out at sea or walking along Carrer Solitari at night and look up to the church, that's what you see.

A huge illuminated Pit Bull terrier sitting on its haunches, snout resting on its paws.

Or is it a Jack Russell?

The hammerhead strikes the sound-bow
ten times twice and four for the quarters,
the Lord calls out to his sons and daughters.

Predictably, they are having none of it.
It's a beautiful day, the year of the lilo,
and the great white Scot basks in the sun

July 30.

Ringing

The eleventh hour of the penultimate day of the first month of
the second semester in the year of our Lord, 2018.

And the end of my lie-in.

The church bells are excruciatingly incessant, they have
been tolling ominously for an hour now.

Perhaps it is finally the long-feared invasion of the reformed
Catholic Unitarian Navy Territorials.

I'm going in.

12.15pm.

I walked the few hundred yards from the apartment up to
the church to find the place eerily deserted except for an elderly
man pottering around the pews. Tall, slightly hunching. Wire-
framed glasses. White hair. Gently illuminated by the golden
glow coming from the light of the baroque altar.

Unusually for me, I decided to try the American approach.

- Hi, good morning sir, my name's Ryan.

141

I held out my hand.

- How do you do?

He shook it. I noted the lack of name response.

- Are you the vicar round here?

- No, I'm just kind of looking after the place.

- Pleased to meet you. I was just wondering what was going on with all these bells.

- What do you mean?

- Well, they haven't stopped for an hour. Is it a special Saint's Day or something?

- Oh, I wouldn't know about that.

That's a bit rich. If there was anyone around here who should know about that surely it was him.

- So, why are they ringing?

- Oh, that will be the computer.

- The computer?

I was beginning to sense that desire to chat and expound, so familiar to all *Cadaquesencs*.

- Yes, in Girona.

- You mean you don't control the bells here in the church?

- No no no, it's automatic. Controlled by a programme somewhere in Girona.

Artificial intelligence enters the vestry. Very Spielberg.

- So when are they programmed for? Well, they toll on the hour, and on the quarters, and for mass.

Didn't really get why they'd spent all morning waking up the bay then.

- But you must be able to control it from here. What do you do when there's a wedding or a funeral?

142

- We have a special button. A timer. But sometimes it goes wrong.

I notice that hint of a wry smile, again.

- Sometimes it just decides to go off and we can't do much about it.

- Can't you call the guys in Girona and get them to turn it off?

- No, it's all computerised, like I said.

- There's no big red button?

- Oh yes, there's a button to stop it. But if we press that then the technicians have to come from Girona to sort it all out.

- So this morning is just a computer error?

- I suppose so.

Funny how it was a pre-mass computer error.

I had my suspicions.

- Strange, well thanks for your time. It's been fascinating. And what did you say your name was again?

- Honesto.

- You're called Honesto? Honest? Really?

And there it was again, that little smile.

- Honesto, yes. And you?

- I'm Ryan.

- Well, have a nice day Ryan. Good morning to you.

JC in prison pending trial, 293 days.

Raholaville

Like most small towns or villages, Cadaqués has its share of clans and dynasties and a social structure which can be easily stratified. The quirk is that these strata are not based solely on money or a typical concept of class. Here, 'class' is also based on longevity. Time is status.

Inevitably, bottom of the pile is the tourist. More than a stratum, they belong in the category of necessary evil. Although there are plenty of locals who will happily point out that when Cadaqués was booming in the 19th century the tourists didn't exist.

It probably wouldn't exist without them now.

Next up is the service class. The recent immigrant, whether Spanish, South American, North African or Barcelonean is considered about as *Cadaquesenc* as a cupcake. No matter if they were born here. They are outsiders brought in to tend the necessary evil. It remains to be seen whether the village will have the power to stamp its salty *Salenc* dialect on the children.

The middle class is made up of two groups in liquid interchangeable positions and, as such, it is not uncommon to find them occasionally inter-breeding: the washed-up bohemian and the newly native can produce very beautiful babies, though the marriages can be shaky. 'Newly native' being anyone who has bought a house here in the last 150 years. 'Washed-up bohemian' including the Swedish gipsy princess stoned in Can Shelabi, and Toby playing his guitar by the lighthouse at sundown.

To be fair, the newly native should be divided into two sub-strata: the simple second-homers and the Catalan bourgeoisie.

The latter are the ones who've given the place some of its stardust.

Monica and I are probably in the category of wannabe second-homers. But we are really just tourists.

Indisputably top of the heap and kings of the hill are the *Pota Negra*, the *Salencs*. Bizarrely named after the most exquisite of cured hams, these are the people whose forebears fought Red Beard and survived the pox.

They include the Faixòs, the Tremols, the Escoffets, the Llorens. They range from the gnarled angry fisherman Pere to the imposing General Escoffet. But the one name which sits astride the town with a legacy longer than the Romanovs' is Rahola.

The only reason their family paper trail stops at 1444 is that the pirates burned the archives. For the last four hundred years, the Rahola dynasty has provided Cadaqués, and Catalonia, with a Facebook's worth of influencers.

Frederic brought the road, the light and the postal service. Victor cured the sick and wrote beautiful poems. Carles was a republican historian and writer assassinated by Franco at the end of the civil war. Another became Catalonia's first ombudsman and defender of the people. Of the current crop, Pilar is an active television commentator and an important loudspeaker in the latest push for independence.

There are no blue plaques. But the roads bear their names. Frederic has a square. Carles and Silvi have streets. Victor's got an avenue. Even the name of the school and the high street are named after Frederic's wife Caritat Serinyana. And the island now called S'Aranella? Used to be *L'illa d'en Rahola*.

145

Maybe they should just be done with it and rename the place Raholaville. After all, some days it does have a kind of Dr Seuss feel.

Dalí could be the Cat in the Hat.

August 2, 2018

What do you reckon to going to communion this later on? *16.32*

When did you get religion? *16.35*

Every time I get on the bus with the mad driver *16.36*

> From the brightened garden of morning's keep,
> a young girl sings at the edge of sleep.
> A slice of sunshine through slatted blinds,
> white sheets and lemons. Time out of mind.

August 2.

Communing

Mmmm. Time out of mind.

I'm not sure I ever got that Dylan title until now.

We have been enveloped by summer. The days drift by without names and we lounge like languid lovers from one long lunch to another. In between, we swim and sunbathe, Monica collects pebbles and I write poems.

We are both looking for that elusive precious gem, and the search is a warm pleasure with the sun on our backs.

Even the village politics seem to have adapted to the summer and adopted the slow-time rhythm of this octopus' garden by the sea.

That said, the situation gets more surreal by the day.

At the entrance to the village there is a small bronze statue called Freedom. a Statue of Liberty but with both arms raised. It is a replica of a little-known Dalí sculpture bequeathed to the town by his secretary John Moore.

It has become a shrine.

A plastic voting urn from the referendum is wedged between her raised hands and the base (a circular tourist information office now in disuse) is covered with photographs of the prisoners, pro-*Republica* posters, and hundreds of yellow ribbons.

Every Wednesday at 8pm, the believers gather in communion.

Yesterday we cycled up before our evening *braves* and beer.

In this heat, evening begins at eight.

There was a small crowd with their heads down, listening intently. They looked strangely like they were being told off. At the centre, the teacher was Pilar Rahola, an over-zealous pro-independence polemicist I have no time for.

As an MP back in the '90s, she had once, infamously, managed to get her car out of the pound after a parking violation by asking a cowering policeman, 'Do you know who you are dealing with?'

Enough said.

I spotted Pep and nodded. I swear his expression said: *Shh, be quiet, this is deadly serious but at the same time highly amusing.*

That is very Pep.

It's an unusual trait among his comrades.

Pilar was saying something about not worrying. That everything that was happening was working in Catalonia's favour. The fact that half the leaders were in jail was not a bad thing in the grander scheme of things. That she had some kind of secret inside knowledge that Europe was going to liberate the nation and its political prisoners.

This time last year, she was partying with the runaway President Puigdemont and the head of the Catalan police force here in Cadaqués. The papers reported them singing *Let it Be* in her garden.

How does that other Beatles song go? 'We would be warm, below the storm. In our little hideaway beneath the waves... resting our head, on the seabed, in an octopus' garden near a cave.'

I think Pilar comes from some long line of Cadaqués Illuminati.

Illuminati as in the Spanish heretics.

Not David Icke's Lizards.

JC in prison pending trial, 296 days.

Murukami's Cats

In Murakami's novel *1Q84,* one of the characters reads a story called 'Town of Cats' in which a young man is travelling around with no particular destination. He just gets on trains, and when he finds somewhere he likes the feel of, he gets off.

One day, he finds himself in a village where everything is closed. All the shops are closed and the shutters are down. Not unlike Cadaqués in winter.

Because there isn't another train until the following day, he is forced to spend the night in the village, and when the sun goes down, he discovers the place is full of cats. All kinds of over-sized cats. Cats opening the bars. Cats sitting at desks writing. Cats dancing, shopping and working.

So he decides to hide in a bell tower (imagine Cadaqués' Santa Maria) and spy on them.

At dawn, all the cats leave, and the place is deserted once again.

The train stops every day at noon and again in the evening. But no one ever gets on, or off. The young man decides to stay for a few days.

On the third night, the cats get wind of him. 'Can't you smell human?' one of them asks. So, they form groups and begin to search. When they realize the smell is coming from the bell tower, they all rush up the stairs. But despite being almost nose to nose, they can't see him and leave.

The young man decides to leave the village but the next day the train doesn't stop. It is as if the young man and the station are not reflected in the eyes of the travellers passing by and he realizes he is lost.

150

'This isn't the town of cats,' he says to himself. It is the place he is destined to be lost in. The train would never stop there again.

Later, when the *New Yorker* asked Murakami what the story was about he said: 'the way a person wanders into a world from which he can never escape, the question of who it is that fills up the empty spaces, the inevitability with which night follows day. Perhaps each of us has his or her own 'town of cats' somewhere deep inside.'

> Heatwaves prowl the alleyways
> to the thrum of air-conditioning

August 7.

Sizzling

Heatwave. This morning I woke up boiling in my own sweat.
If it wasn't because I know she loves me so much, I might have
thought Monica was trying to kill me: tricking me into sleeping
with the windows open and leaving the aircon off (something
which has been impossible for the last week) and then, at some
point, getting up, quietly closing the windows and turning on
the heating.

I jerked awake like I'd been poked with a cattle prod and
ran straight into the shower. 3.49am. 30ºC.

I figured at this point trying to get back to sleep was
pointless, so I decided to get dressed and try to catch the classic
Cadaqués sunrise over Caials.

Unlike the evenings, which disappear quickly into the night
as the sun drops down behind the Pení, the dawn endures. The
light is mineral, like the Clarendon filter on Instagram. It's
worth the effort.

After some tea and toast, I found myself walking up the
rastell-cobble streets towards the church. The *rastell* is unique
to Cadaqués. The dark slate is slotted vertically into the
ground. Originally it was done to give the donkeys a good
foothold. Now it was sweating in the heat.

The village was eerie. Hot moonlight. Still, and tropical.
All the windows and doors of the houses were wide open and

there was a soft silence, punctuated by the occasional cough or the odd snore. It was the strangest feeling. Like walking in and out of a collective dream.

It got even stranger as I approached the church and saw the cats.

Two were sitting on top of a darkened carpet of ivy and bougainvillea which covered a nearby ruined shack. Another was perched on a stone wall licking its coat. There were four more sitting motionless in various doorways. And in the window of the very last house, a huge white Persian caught briefly in the moonlight, was staring out of the window. Right at me.

I felt like the man in Murakami's town of cats. There was even a bell tower.

I sat down on the wall under the cypress tree in front of the church, surrounded by the cats, and looked out as first light moved slowly across the cape like a tide of pink mercury.

I got that feeling again. The amazing feeling, that sometimes, in Cadaqués, magic really does exist.

I'll forgive Monica for having tried to cook me.

JC in prison pending trial, 301 days.

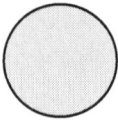

El Gato Azul (The Blue Cat)

Number 30 of 92 restaurants in Cadaqués

Dinah
Tugley
Wood
👍 3

'Spot the cats...'

A hidden jewel. Second time here. It's just down from that crazy cats' home by the church.
The wine list has some great local wines. Nothing crazy expensive.
The owner and his wife Richard & Isabelle are hands on. Isabelle is cooking amazing delicacies in the kitchen. Richard is hosting and taking care in the dining room.
The first night I had an eggplant toast with Emmenthal cheese, peppers and a touch of oregano. Super satisfying and delicious! The wine was great. House wine. I got it chilled with an ice cube as it's a heat wave here...32 today. Maybe hotter tomorrow.
Tonight, I ordered the El Gato Azul Platter: Kebbe, falafel, tabbouleh, hummus, baba ghanoush, dolmades, pitta bread. Life is great. Richard plays cool music. Do not miss this magic spot.
It's all reasonably priced and the cat-themed space is crazy cute. On the walls, on the serviettes everywhere miaow miaow miaow. Their menu even has a gallery on the cover of famous people with their cats.
See how many you can spot. Miaow.

Date of visit: July, 2018

You can take a horse to water...

In Cadaqués, like most coastal villages, the sea is omnipresent. Its reflective light pours in through every misshaped window. On stormy days its wind-whipped waves snap at the heels of passers-by. And its deep bay has provided a centuries-long source of wealth.

But the town's relationship with fresh water has been more problematic. *Aigua dolça*, sweet water, as they call it here.

Even though during cloudbursts rivers of the stuff flood down from the hills at 100 litres per second, smashing bridges and carrying away cars, its drinkability is only a recently won luxury.

Up until the 1950s, it was common to see women using *dolls* to carry water from the old well on their heads and some of the locals still refer to the drinking water as *aigua de doll.*

It's hard to square this image of women balancing Grecian-style amphoras on their heads with the modernity of Dalí's lobster telephone. Like sitting in an outside lavatory and checking your Instagram feed.

There are a couple of sculptures commemorating these ladies on either side of the bay and they still organize a *doll* race during the annual village *festa major* in September. But by 1951 the local council had decided that women with pots on their heads weren't quite the image of modernity that Franco's dictatorship should be projecting. And fascist dictator or not, Franco was good at water. He was responsible for most of Spain's hydroelectric network.

Maybe with a little help from the thousands of Republican prisoners who did the heavy lifting.

So, the council got everyone together and explained the project of supplying the houses with fresh water from the well using a system of pumps. The villagers were worried. After all, this is a place that did pretty well without a road until the end of the 19th century. Plumbing? Makes you soft.

Legend has it that one of the fishermen asked what would happen if the well ran dry and then became filled with salt-water. We'll add some sugar, they answered.

By 1954, the village was plumbed. But that fisherman hadn't been wrong. With the increase of the crowds in summer, the well ran dry, and the water came out of the taps salty. Following some awkward years when drinking water was sold from the back of a truck and then later supplied by a huge water tanker which would moor in the bay during the summer months, it wasn't until 1972 when the issue was finally resolved by piping fresh water in from Castelló d'Empúries.

They might have easily fixed the problem by building a collector at the end of the storm drain that comes out next to the Casino. It is here the summer storms that run off the steep rocky slopes and down through the village are channelled into the sea. And it is here the first bridge, a beautiful stone-built double arch, was taken out in 1921 by Storm Hemaia.

The villagers took advantage of the stones to build a bench in the nearby square. It became known as *el banc d'en sinofos*, 'the bench for the lazy'. It is still there today.

With the arrival of the second bridge, the villagers' bums were soon spoilt for choice. The walls were wide enough to sit on comfortably and it became a popular spot for sitting in the dock of the bay...

Unfortunately, it only lasted until 1982, when it too succumbed to the force of the water.

The current bridge, an unattractive benchless structure of cement and iron, looks strong enough. Strange though, that the height of the pebbled beach, bayside, means that even just a robust shower leaves visitors needing waders to reach their cars.

The cars they left there to avoid the charges in the municipal car park.

It is not inconceivable that the pebbly incline is man-made.

> Lightning flashes over the bay
> catching a pair of midnight swimmers by surprise.
> They run for cover, shrieking, holding hands
> delighting in the novelty of their silvery tans.

August 8.

Storming

When the cloud burst, it happily caught us in L'Estable eating our way through one of their enormous plates of tiny green peppers. Sensing the imminent rain, we had taken a window seat inside and enjoyed a front-line view of skidding waiters and sprinting tourists illuminated by huge flashes of sheet lightning.

In front of us, a group of Russians decided to brave it out under the canvas sun umbrella on the terrace. It took about three minutes before they were standing next to our table, soggy and dripping.

When the storm quietened, we settled the bill and walked up the Riba Pitxot, past the empty tables and folded-up chairs. The lightning had moved out to sea and flashed intermittently in the dark like a slow-motion stroboscope. It was still spitting, and the tiny restaurants were packed with scores of diners standing, huddled together, waiting to get back outside. Everyone was laughing and smiling. This unexpected drama was fun.

In Talla, it looked like an impromptu party as waiters squeezed through the crowd with trays loaded with tapas and glasses of cava. Now *that* is customer service.

This morning I decided to go and inspect the storm damage.

158

Hopefully, a new Porsche stuck under the bridge. Hopefully not, a sea full of debris.

Not much going on.

No car dramas. And the water was crystalline, although the sea had spewed seaweed onto the beaches.

Perhaps these unwelcoming piles of kelp had encouraged the proliferation of the village's *manteras*: the small, beautiful and obviously well-kept little girls playing shopkeepers alongside the beach. They were selling an array of painted rocks, shells and home-made friendship bracelets which they had spread out on tiny pieces of cloth.

It's not that they needed the money, that's for sure. Half of them are the daughters of Catalonia's elite. It's just play. And they are small and cute. Which is obviously why they don't get moved on or fined. Even if there is a sign prohibiting pedlars: *Venda ambulant prohibit.*

I call them *manteras* like the *manteros* in Barcelona. The *manteros* are the groups of Africans who play cat and mouse with the local police. Their goods, anything from fake Nikes to selfie sticks, are laid out on blankets which can be quickly converted into bags if they need to run – which is often. Those guys DO get moved on.

The Spanish for blanket is *manta*, hence the name. The suffixes *-as* or *-os* are gender markers. The semantic similarity and the cloths laid out on the floor are all they have in common. Except for their DNA, which is 99.9% identical.

Still, it's all about the 0.1%, right?

Shame about that Porsche.

JC in prison pending trial, 301 days.

159

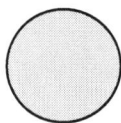 Talla

Number 2 of 92 restaurants in Cadaqués

MississippiMik
Manchester, UK **'Rain or shine'**

👍881

Come rain or shine, every time I come back here, I always look forward to eating at Talla! You know what...it never ever disappoints. The great views over Cadaqués and the view of those three arches where Dalí painted that painting...the staff are super nice...smart, elegant and eager to please. Good-looking too. And the food? WOW! It is too low key for a Michelin star which I love about this place but in my humble opinion, foodwise they are Michelin rock stars. These guys rock on!

My favourites are: the cuttlefish croquettes, truffle/foie omelette, chicken/foie cannelloni and the Tiramisu.

Date of visit: August,2018

Talking salty

Insular, quirky, profoundly connected to the sea, and dating back centuries. Why would the language be any different?

Thanks to its relative isolation for the last millennium, the locals have managed to maintain a peculiar dialect, peppered with phrases and expressions indecipherable for most outsiders. That includes their neighbours from nearby Figueres.

Known as *salat*, or salty, its musicality – also common to the Balearic Islands and further down the coast around Begur – is marked by the use of *es, so, sa, sos,* and *ses* as articles. You can see this in some of the names around Cadaqués: the restaurant *Sa Gambina* or the shop *Sa Botiga*.

But what really differentiates *Cadaquesencs* from the people next door is their lexicon which, unsurprisingly, is mostly made up of words and sayings related to the weather, the wind, the sea and fish. Especially fish.

They might have as many ways of describing wind as the Todzhu people of Siberia have of naming reindeer (13 alone to describe reindeer with different ages) but molluscs, crustaceans and pretty much anything found in the water provide the bulk of the unofficial *Cadaquesenc* dictionary.

Futarro describes something useless (*futarra* being the worthless fish thrown away by the fishermen), and men with deep voices are described as seashell horns (*fisicorn*). If you *fas ulls de pixota* you've got the eyes of a hake and look a bit ill, while *Qui dorm no pesca* 'he who sleeps gets no fish' is a variation on the early bird catching the worm.

My favourite?

És una estolta: he's a bit of a squid.

> Look at what he's carrying, drunk as a barrel
> talking between himself, walking around the branches.
> He comes over to me. God how he falls me badly
> taking my hair and eating my coconut.
> Speaking up to his elbows.

August 3.

Losing my language

Arrived back after four days in Edinburgh.

Mid-August anywhere on the Costa Brava is uncomfortably full. Here, it's not uncommon for the local police to send cars back up the hill because there's no space. This, combined with my need for a regular injection of the English spoken word, made four days at the festival a *sí o sí* proposition. That's 'yes or yes'.

Edinburgh was cool and fresh. Cadaqués is humid. The village is heaving, and my head is still full of the festival. I'm looking forward to a good night's sleep and reclaiming my thoughts, which are currently drowned out by notions of self, identity, and nationhood.

Curious how both Brexit and the Catalan independence push share similar fault lines. There are traits of Brexiteers I can see in the *Cadaquesencs* too. Terribly, I think Farage would fit right in. It's the uglier side of *nos amb nos*.

But these people... these people (*que volen aquesta gent?*) who muse on their nationality. I wonder.

When I see the comedian Ahir Shah shouting jokes about his Britishness but being weighed down by his Indian baggage, or the China Plate theatre company toying with the idea of the impossibility of trying to shed your nationality, how it marks you indelibly. I wonder.

Here I am in my faithless church after 25 years, and I wonder. I have lost one nationality without gaining another. And something similar is happening to my language. As my native voice fades away and I find myself grasping for words, my newfound tongue remains strange, yet familiar.

I am envious of the way the locals here have maintained their archaic, salty dialect of Catalan. The almost historical purity of their language. Clearly, the less you move and the less you are invaded, the better it is for your linguistic survival.

Over the years, my English has been invaded, colonialized and forced to interbreed. Soon after my arrival, there was a frighteningly quick descent into the use of that Antipodean 'yeah' at the end of every other sentence. A meaningless *nada* 'nothing' began to appear willy nilly between sentences. Fragments of local culture and everyday turns of phrase soon attached themselves to their linguistic host.

If my native language was bark, the most untranslatable parts of Catalan became the fungus.

Now I am lost in translation. That question from before? *Que volen aquesta gent?* What do they want these people? I tend to throw it around every time I don't understand someone or essentially disapprove of an opinion. It's a rhetorical question from an old song by the Mallorcan singer Maria Mar del Bonet about the death of an anarchist in police custody during the end years of Franco's rule. The phrase was soon picked up by the Catalans and indicates a mixture of disbelief, scorn and desperation every time the Spanish nationalist right make an inflammatory comment about Catalonia. Its current usage is limited and implies political allegiance, a sense of belonging and saves at least another six sentences.

If the freestyle adoption of local phrases, inappropriate translation and the slapstick neologizing I especially enjoy with my boys (whose bilingualism allows for the impossible) weren't enough to make me indecipherable: the combination of lentition in Catalan – in which the consonants become more resonant – and the vowel reduction common to English, means I have developed what can only be described as a musical mumble.

As time passes, I am becoming almost unintelligible and our family mealtimes are like a gathering of the Ethiopian Ongota speakers of whom there are only six left in the world.

Nos amb nos doesn't even come close.

JC in prison pending trial, 306 days.

Gone with the wind

The *rosa dels vents* (the wind rose) originates from a heraldic motif, the fleur-de-lis. It is a compass. A simple star-like image imbued with the mystery and magic of the winds that inspired it. Something you could imagine as the insignia of the rebel alliance. Star Wars, not Brexit.

Unsurprisingly, given the Cadaqués maritime tradition (and its penchant for rebel-alliancing?) there are several of these compasses painted on the walls around the village. There is also one, laid out in dark cobblestone, in Plaça Estrella – Star Square.

They could have saved themselves the bother.

A rudimentary dagger would have sufficed.

A knife with the letter T at its tip would have done the trick.

You might think the banter over *braves* would be all about the *vent del Llevant,* coming in off the sea, wrecking boats onto rocks and making it near impossible to sail out of the bay. Or the humid *vent de la Passi* that carries in a ghostly sea fret during Holy Week. Or perhaps, the *vent del Xaloc* that rains dirty red

165

Saharan mud onto the pretty white façades of the houses and the shiny decks of fibreglass boats.

But no. In Cadaqués, the only talk in town is the Tramuntana.

The locals have almost as many words and sayings related to this wind as the Italians have for pasta. *Tramuntana Fina* is a soft wind accompanied by good weather; the *Tramuntana Gallinera* (chicken wind) blows during the day but relents at night; *Tramuntana, vent de gana* is a rhyming hungry wind.

From the Latin *transmuntanus,* beyond the mountain, this powerful north wind gathers force as it accelerates over the Northern Pyrenees and often hits the Empordà with speeds of up to 200km an hour.

Vladimir Nabokov referred to its violence in his story *Le Mepris,* and Gabriel Garcia Marquez said it was a wind so harsh that 'even your best friends look at you with hostility.'

Sometimes lasting up to eight days straight, statistics show that in Cadaqués it blows an average of 155 days a year.

In an average week, that's Saturday, Sunday and Monday with the flaps down.

Year-round madness. And it's not just the dogs.

Tocats per la Tramuntana, 'touched' by the wind (mad as hatters). *Atramuntanats,* bananas. *Quan bufa la Tramuntana, tothom es trastorna,* when the wind blows, your mind goes. Some of the most popular Catalan expressions for bonkers are tied to this beast and are frequently used to refer to the *Cadaquesencs* themselves.

It was fear of being driven mad by the Tramuntana that led Dalí's grandad Galo to pack his bags and leave for Barcelona. Sadly, he must have taken some of it with him in his suitcase.

He still ended up jumping out of a window at the age of 37 in 1886. And perhaps, Salvador himself warded off this fear by behaving as if he were mad.

But what really is ludicrous, in these ecological end times, is that this monster of a wind doesn't generate a single watt of electricity in Cadaqués or Cap de Creus. Unlike over the border where it feeds wind turbines in Ribesaltes, Òpol and Centernac.

In the Languedoc, there are over 200 generators milking the Tramuntana for all its worth.

Here? Not even a wind chime.

Not yet anyway.

But that may be about to change.

The wind chime, that is.

Salvador Dalí's dream of building an organ powered by the wind, *l'Orgue de la Tramuntana,* came a step closer to realization when the local council in nearby Vilajuïga announced plans to resurrect the project in Quermançó Castle.

A representative of the Catalan Government in the region, Pere Vila, said: 'All the administrations should work together and add our grain of sand to make this project a reality. Something that would be very good for the country.'

Tocats per la Tramuntana.

167

> Parasols become javelins, tables are kites
> skiffs turn to shrapnel, kayaks are knives.
> One man, on a lilo, dies.

August 14.

Howling

I woke up at 3.49 and the infamous Tramuntana wind was blowing with a vengeance. At first, I thought the neighbours were moving furniture until I realized the infernal noise was the canvas we have been using as an awning to protect us from the sun. It had been caught in the gale and was snapping and flapping in the gusts.

For a while, I lay there imagining us being lifted up over the bay. The apartment under sail, slipping anchor and flying off into the night sky and through constellations. Then, practicalities kicked in. If one of those metal toggles snapped, it could break a window. Or kill a cat.

It wasn't long before I was standing naked on the roof of the building in a force 9 gale. Full moon. *Double entendre.*

I've said before, our terrace is like a room that has been dug out of the roof of the building by a JCB, and the structure that supports the awning is a rectangular cast iron frame. Due to the incline of the roof, the toggles nearest the kitchen can be unhooked by standing on a stool. The ones further away require standing on the edge of the roof and gripping onto the frame.

On a sunny day with a mild breeze, this can be an enjoyable activity combining a gentle feeling of daring with spectacular views over the bay. Monica is always telling me to be careful, but I think she is possibly more worried about the tiles than my wellbeing. Unless I've had a couple. Then I think she fears me scooting off over the rooftops for the fun of it.

It is tempting.

What is no fun is being naked in a gale in the middle of the night clinging on for your life and trying desperately to hold the canvas which you have managed to unhook from three of the toggles and now, on the roof edge, struggling with the last which is, due to Murphy's elementary law of physics, being an absolute pain in the ass.

The sail is 12ft by 12ft. Unwieldy. But yes, in the end, I worked it free.

Then it flew away.

The Tramuntana whipped it out of my hands as soon as I'd unhooked the last toggle. Off it went in the direction of the sea, like a crisp packet on a breeze.

The Tramuntana might make the fish happier and the bread rise better, but there was no metaphysical joy here. No magical boat trip through Cassiopeia and the celestial spheres. Just me, naked. Howling at the moon. *Tocat per la Tramuntantana.*

In Port Doguer at nine am, the wind was still going strong. It was a fist. The air screamed narrow and the sea looked as if it was draining away from the shore as fast as possible.

I had this brief vision of the whole bay emptied. Just boulders and stones, maybe the odd trunk of pirates' treasure leaking gold coins, the barnacled hull of a galleon. A huge quarry with the buoys transformed into balloons in the sky, tugging at their rusty chains.

It was no weather for a swim.

So, I turned back to come home, and there it was. Snug, between the upturned boats that lay on the shingle like beached whales. A silver toggle glinting in the sunlight.

Almost winking.

JC in prison pending trial, 307 days.

Salvador, and friends – The Cadaqués Palette.

In Dalí's theme park house in Port Lligat there is a mirror in the bedroom, angled to the window. You might think that this was so he could lie in bed and watch the sun come up, but the surrealist writer Rene Crevel claimed it was really because Dalí wanted to wake up every morning bathed in sunlight. Like a mythical creature. A God.

He is certainly omnipresent.

The tourist office promotes a 'Dalí on foot' route where a dozen perspex panels with Dalí reproductions offer you the chance to stand on the spot where the great man painted a particular picture, although to be fair, they really need to put a perspex sheet over the whole village: Dalí didn't so much paint Cadaqués as use its geography and melting rock formations as background in most of his paintings.

Every other café or bar seems to have a photograph: Dalí with the owner. Dalí watching Duchamp play chess. Dalí in a Mad-Hatter pose. Dalí eating ice cream flamboyantly. Dalí twirling his moustache. These days he would be using a selfie-stick as a cane. Even the cats' home by the church has a photograph of him in the window. Pretty strange considering he once said, 'I love cats. I love to swing them around by the tail.'

Half the village claims to have worked for him, and everybody knew him. Dionísis' dad mended his boats, Anita prepared his prawns, Vicentet contributed to his oeuvre by shooting one of his paintings, and Joan was carpenter and unofficial photographer. The Hotel Residencia website boasts of having more original works by Dalí than his own House Museum in Port Lligat.

But you don't hear many people talking about what a great guy he was. In fact, some of the locals are still fuming that his big mouth ruined their chance to claim compensation after the big freeze killed off the area's olive trees in 1956. Apparently, he managed to save his own trees and then told the agricultural ministry that everyone else's would be fine too. They weren't.

His relationship with part of his family was a disaster and his relationship with half of his friends wasn't much better. His father stopped speaking to him after Dalí said there was nothing he liked better than spitting on his dead mother's portrait. He didn't speak to his sister for forty years due to his wife Gala's jealousy or vice versa (it's rumoured his sister Anna-Maria unsuccessfully tried to get Gala arrested for polygamy). Luis Buñuel fell out with him over his flirtation with the post-war Franco regime and when his great friend/lover Lorca was shot by the fascists he simply said, 'Ole!' and went on to criticize him for being a homosexual. A bit rich coming from someone who, we know now, didn't much care which way the wind blew.

Clearly, he was a piece of work. But he was a piece of work whose presence as an international superstar artist brought a steady trail of admirers and acolytes to the village including Walt Disney and the Duke of Windsor. It also encouraged scores of other artists to visit, such as René Magritte, David Hockney, Richard Hamilton and cinema director and collaborator Buñuel.

Those big names meant Cadaqués became a delicious self-fulfilling prophecy. It's the standard rule of gentrification: first come the artists, then come the buyers, then come the wannabes and then, boom! You've got a scene.

Catherine Moore, the widow of Dalí's manager, the late Captain John Moore, explained that they opened the first gallery, Galeria Es Portal, at the beginnings of the 70s. 'The mayor at the time said "you're crazy. nobody's going to buy any pictures here". Two or three years later there were fourteen galleries, and every Saturday during the summer, people would dress up and visit them all.'

The truth is, since then, a lot of the smaller artists have been priced out. But a dozen galleries remain. Up to 60 artists continue to live and work in the village. Catherine Moore is still a practising 'patron of the arts', renting out large spaces at peppercorn rents to a handful of artists she describes as her protégés.

No lesser a truth is that although Dalí and his entourage might have brought the modern world to the village, they didn't bring art. That honour goes to Ramon Pichot.

Towards the end of the 19th century, the well-known impressionist painter Pichot possibly became Cadaqués' first tourist and second-home owner when he built his house in Es Sortell, the outcrop of rock between Llane beach and Sa Conca.

The estate went on to become the setting for a notorious bohemian bourgeois dynasty, regularly visited by politicians and artists of the day. Joan Miró, Andre Derain, the cellist Pau Casals, the composer Enric Granados and the Republican politician Mañuel Azaña were all guests at Es Sortell, and it was Pichot who organized Picasso's summer visit in 1910.

A good fifty years before Dalí himself bought his fisherman's shack in Port Lligat, the only hipsters in town were the Pichots. At the time, whenever the villagers – who were still carrying water jugs on their heads and spent most of their days mending fishing nets – saw a well-dressed townie walking about they would say, 'Look, there goes a Pichot.'

Dalí's dad returned to his family roots and bought a second home in Cadaqués and when the twenty-something Salvador returned to Cadaqués to paint, Pichot was an early influence. His nephew, the painter Antoni Pitxot became a contemporary of Dalí's; some might even say a friend.

The real question should be what exactly attracted Pichot, Dalí, Picasso, Magritte and all the others to make the effort to reach this remote island of a town in the first place. The answer is the Cadaqués palette.

When Dalí talks about the minerality of the place, or Josep Pla mentions its liquid silence, what they are describing are just different facets of the Cadaqués palette: the influence of geography and light; the unique alloy of colour, texture and light which illuminates these painters' canvasses with the effervescence of difference. It's as if this palette has an extra bit of magic.

You doubt Picasso and Derain came up with Cubism while staring out at the lineal mash-up that is Es Baluard? Just look at those paintings, look at the village. Look at the dates. Of course Dalí's melting watches and Angel Planell's amorphous landscapes are the metamorphic rocks of the Cap de Creus. Matisse's famous azure? Tramuntana blue.

In the work of today's artists, it might be the pink murmur in Shigeyoshi Koyama's seascapes, the blinding white zinc of José Luis Scaffo's skies or the comic swagger of Javier Aznarez's curves, some of which are illustrating this book!

If the Cadaqués palette were a soap powder it would wash whiter than white, if it were a brand of cosmetics it would be because you're worth it, and if it were a cereal, it would be the breakfast of champions.

> A fine pink mist hangs over the bay,
> the sea shimmers like a lake of rosé wine.

August 18.

Musing

Bar Estic, again, and the sunset softens Es Baluard with a tinge of lavender.

At the table next to me a pretty young man, long black hair, early twenties, is doing a charcoal sketch of a grizzled older man, grey beard, early forties. I'm tempted to think lover/student/master but it's more likely family/son/father. Either way, it's uncanny.

Today the weather has been surprisingly fresh. The Tramuntana turned cold and there have been soft showers on and off for most of the day. (Late summer already?) A perfect time then, to visit the Cadaqués Museum which I (embarrassingly) still haven't done. I was never convinced enough to pay the entrance fee of five euros.

Shame on me.

It's also very odd that the Cadaqués Museum is solely about painters when the village has so much interesting history that isn't art. And so many local historians too.

One colourful character, Juan Manuel Tajadura Ijalba, who used to be the local dustman, has compiled an impressive archive of historical documents dating back to the 13th century. It is like the missing archive burnt by Red Beard.

He also has collection of scale models of all the boats that have been shipwrecked off the coast.

176

No matter. The local council can't find a space for any of it. Shame on them.

So, here is this one museum is tucked away at the back end of the old town. It has a yawningly predictable picture of Dalí on one of the outside walls – sometimes you wonder whether anyone else ever lived here – but is ostensibly dedicated to all the artists who have had a connection with the village throughout its history. And there have been a lot. This place is St Ives to the power of ten.

The cultural offer relies on donations, often from the artists themselves, their hedge fund managers, or their legacy lawyers. From what I could see, most of them are pretty stingy considering what they took from the place and what they have given back.

There were a few Dalí prints, a couple of sad Picasso drawings and some photographs of his painting 'The Port of Cadaqués'. No mention that he might well have invented cubism that summer of 1910, looking out from his window across to the church, in his trademark stripy t-shirt, mug of coffee in hand. Then again, that might just be my theory. The timing's right though.

There were plenty of other interesting pictures, including a print of Richard Hamilton's church altar collage and a phenomenal Pitxot stone lady who looked like a Lucien Freud take on Ironman. Of the other big hitters, I couldn't see anything from Duchamp or any references to Magritte's Surrealist classic 'Threatening Weather', which depicts the Tramuntana and uses the bay as its backdrop.

But sitting on the stairs, flicking through a reference book, I did discover it was here that Hamilton and Dieter Roth hatched their idea of an exhibition for dogs.

Inspired by a local stray called Sparky Luis, the paintings had included images of sausages and old boots. When it opened at the Galeria de Cadaqués in 1976 there was even a special section for dogs where the paintings were exhibited at dog eye-level. The private view included bone-shaped biscuits and bowls of water.

When we left the museum, it had started to drizzle, and we got caught up in one of those terrifying group itinerary events which usually make me want to run for cover. This one was about the history of the old town. Not uninteresting, but in the company of another fifty people in cagoules? No thanks.

Monica insisted.

I tagged along with a grimace and a sulk.

We discovered our apartment was right next to where the old cemetery had been before it was moved out of town in compliance with the 18th century plague laws.

The guide claimed that all the remains were exhumed but I'll bet there's still the odd bone buried around here somewhere. Or a misplaced skull. And even if they had managed to comb the place with the meticulousness of an FBI forensic team, ghosts don't move.

We have been sleeping among the dead for the last six months.

More happily, I also discovered that 'British artist Richard Hamilton lived in this house (behind the church) which had once belonged to the Count of Empúries'.

This would have suited the aristocratic Hamilton and got me thinking of a sketch of him done by David Hockney which I'd just seen in the book in the museum: ratty-haired Hamilton, grizzled beard, cigar between his fingers, sits louche on a basket-weave chair. The very same type of chair as the one suspended in Magritte's painting.

Was Hockney making a point? Threatening weather...?

Hockney and his partner Peter Schlesinger, came to Cadaqués in 1971, invited by his friend Mark Lancaster who'd rented an apartment from Teeny Duchamp. And it was here that the relationship ended.

The two had been arguing for some months before. Schlesinger had met the painter Eric Boman and Hockney was getting jealous. To try and patch up the situation, Hockney suggested a trip to the South of France, then on to Barcelona to see the Picasso museum, taking in a few days in Cadaqués on the way back.

Lancaster, who had no idea what was going on between the two men, invited Boman too.

Bad move.

The holiday was a disaster.

Finding himself with Boman and a whole group of English people invited by Jonathan Guinness, and having to put up with Richard Hamilton's legendarily corrosive humour, was a particularly unpleasant experience for Hockney. One day it blew up.

Guinness had invited them all for a trip around Cap de Creus on his boat, but Hockney was having none of it and said he wasn't going. Nobody paid him any attention. On the day of the trip, Boman recalled a shouting match on the shore.

179

Hockney was crying. He shouted, imploring, 'If you go, don't bother coming back.'

Hamilton was laughing and shouting.

The cruellest kind of revellery.

Artist in the sloop, three sheets to the wind.

Hockney insisted, screaming out, 'I'm going, come with me.'

Schlesinger stayed.

End of.

And now, here I am, up on the *Riba*. The very same spot, with my half-filled cup, as the younger boy draws the older man.

Uncanny.

JC in prison pending trial, 310 days.

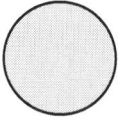

El Barroco

Number 42 of 92 restaurants in Cadaqués

BillThackaray
Basildon
👍 17

'Magical, bohemian, historical'

We arrived in Cadaqués a little bit late and wanted to eat but something different in this arty little town. We couldn't have chosen better. When we got to the restaurant there was a bohemian patio where, according to the owner Sami, Dalí and his friends used to eat. Sami said Dalí designed the logo. Sami is a great host and an artist too, there are lots of his paintings around the place. After dinner he played the piano for us, something we really enjoyed.

The tables are all old Singer sewing machine tables and we got a table by the fireplace which made everything seem more romantic. The food was delicious. Best falafel I've ever tried, hummus was brilliant and the mutubal even better. Obviously, there was loads of mint tea and those typical Lebanese cakes. And all for 76 euros including the tip!

Finally, I'd just like to thank the group of Americans at the next table for sharing their intimate conversation with us and making our evening.

Date of visit: August, 2018

On the Rocks

An advert from 1962 for the construction company Kulip S.A. reads: 'In a unique European countryside, Dantesque geography of amazing contrasts. The efforts of three companies have made possible the urban development of 5,000,000 sq. metres and opened to the world a land isolated and untouched during thousands of years.'

Thanks for that.

A dramatic rocky headland steeped in myth and malevolence, the Cap de Creus is the furthest point east of the Iberian Peninsula. At the very tip of this furthest point east lies the tiny Illa de Massa d'Or, the Isle of Gold, the first place to be touched by the rays of the rising sun.

The island is said to have transformative powers, the rock is also said to confer immortality. But the hundreds of rocky outcrops and underwater canyons around the Cape tell a different story: a story of Phoenician shipwrecks, sunken treasure and terrible deaths. The reefs of Cap de Creus have been a maritime graveyard and a sailors' curse for centuries. Hence the name: Cape of Crosses.

Cala Culip is especially fertile terrain for divers in search of lost treasures. The wrecks of several Roman corbitas have been found in this north-facing cove, tricked by the apparent protection it offered from all the winds except the one that mattered: the Tramuntana.

Closer to Cadaqués, it was on the reef of s'Aranella that the the Douaumont, a French ship, sank in 1920 during a violent storm. Although most of the crew were saved (except for a Senegalese sailor who was strangled by the rescue rope), the force of the waves split the boat open like a pomegranate, liberating its cargo. A century later, the beaches are still speckled with tiny opaque pebbles of *rosso corsa*: all that's left of its 4,000 tonnes of roof-red tiles.

And it was just eight nautical miles off this coast that a German U-boat torpedoed the British steamer the Llanishen (Richard Duck & Co, Stockton on Tees) on August 8th, 1917.

The Greek divers brought in for the salvage operation said there were no signs of the mermaids and lobster palaces they'd been told to expect.

A bane for some, a boon for others. During Cadaqués' lean years, the plethora of hidden coves and the difficulty of their navigation meant that the area became rife with smugglers. Only the locals knew the ins and outs of the fjord-like inlets and more importantly, the secret paths that led to them. As Catalan writer Josep Pla says in his short story *Pa i Raim*: 'The conditions this land has for this type of work are extraordinary. Unique. The constant possibility of creating a convincing feint means they can never guess your intentions from land.'

All that's left from that era of coastal cat and mouse is the grand ochre building, built for the *carrabiners* – the earliest customs police in the area – on the very top of Cap de Creus next to the lighthouse In 1910. It's now a restaurant run by an Englishman called Chris selling chicken curry and staffed by dope-smoking millennials dressed like smugglers, living the dream. The views from here are astounding as the Pyrenees pour down into the ultramarine and the cape reaches out into the Mediterranean like a gnarled giant's hand staking its claim.

Over the years wind and water erosion have created bizarre forms in the rocks. The most celebrated of these can be found

183

in the Pla de Tudela, and from looking at these bizarre sculptures in the rock it's easy to see where Dalí got his inspiration for his melting landscapes. As Ian Gibson said in *The Shameful Life of Salvador Dalí*: 'It is a vast natural theatre of optical illusions.'

Until very recently, Pla de Tudela was in the private hands of the French-owned Club Med who bought exclusive access to the area in 1964 as part of Franco's push to increase tourism. The rumorology at the time said that his brother-in-law made a mint.

The end result was that the scenery was subsequently ruined by 400 bungalows where Western Europe's free young things could strut their stuff and hang loose, far from the disapproving eyes of the continent's last remaining dictator, or the envious villagers.

Fortunately, in 2004 a combination of new coastal laws and a failing business model allowed a simple compromise. The Spanish government bought them out for a few million, demolished the bungalows and used the 44,000 cubic metres of rubble to build a new marina in nearby Roses.

The Pla de Tudela, Cala Culip and the rest of Cap de Creus is now a protected national park. The smugglers paths are hiking trails, the ships' graveyards are full of luxury yachts 'cove hopping', and there are no discussions about going topless. Around here, the Emperor's new clothes are the hottest thing going.

> Moon was peeking in through Dawn's window.
> He saw Day putting on her best bikini,
> getting ready for the beach.
> Moon stormed off in a sulk

August 22.

Undressing

Bikini banter.

One of the funnier things about the pebbled coves and spiky slate sun decks around Cap de Creus is the gentle but continual tension between nudists and non-nudists.

As a general rule, the further away the cove from Cadaqués Central, the more rights for the naked. In fact, in the more inaccessible places like Cala Tavallera, keeping your kit on can generate serious frowning. Well, not exactly frowning, because these laid-back carefree dudes and dudesses do not frown. They just emanate negative swimming togs vibes.

Some of them can be quite in your face about it.

Personally, I have issues. Depending on the competition, I can feel intimidated. Depending on the bodies, I can feel put off.

Typical masculine hang-up conundrum due to faulty social conditioning. I know. But if it's just Monica and me, I'm happy to throw caution to the wind, hang loose and jump in for a bit of shark fishing using my manhood for bait.

Today there was a striking example of this gentle tension between pro and anti-disrobers in s'Alquerira Gran. This lovely cove, around the corner from the Dalí theme park in Port Lligat, is close enough to both civilization and nature to ensure

186

an interesting mix of well-groomed picnickers and well-hung wildlings.

At the entrance to the cove, someone has daubed *platja nudista* (nudist beach) in red paint across the stony ground. This has been subsequently crossed out in yellow paint by someone else – or possibly the same person with an interesting sense of humour – who has written *platja familiar* (family beach).

Red and yellow. The two colours of the Spanish flag. Or the Catalan flag. Depending on which way you hang.

I wonder if having diametrically opposed opinions about things, including sunbathing, is what's *de rigueur* in this part of the world. Although it's probably just a sign of the times everywhere in this young and angry century.

Anyway, as we walked down towards the cove, I could see scores of naked people splayed out on the left side of the beach and others perched on the rocks out to sea. Many of them were reading. This would have been an odd enough sight in itself, but on the right-hand side, sat a large group of young Muslim girls in burkinis, covered from head to toe in skin-tight lycra. Wetsuits designed by Chanel. Ninja super-heroes for the Me-too movement.

Neither group seemed particularly conflicted by the other, but you knew they had considered each other. At least once. Guaranteed.

What bothered me then, and still bothers me now, is that in this age of 'live-porn-streamed-to-your-pre-teens-bedroom', I'm not quite sure which group represents progress.

JC in prison pending trial, 314 days.

Us with Us

Darwin on the rocks

In the igneous library
the naked readers
squat on rocks,
book in hand.
They flaunt the line
passed down
from chimp to man:
there is grandeur
in this view of life.

Cue typewriters, apes
the complete works
infinite time.
And all that jazz.

1970something

It was a warm summer night and L'Hostal was heaving with wannabes, has-beens and those who really are. The notorious bar was momentarily the centre of the fantasy universe that was the 1970s. There were so many different poles of attraction that the gleaming milieu of Barcelona's jet set was in danger of being torn apart by the gravitational pull of so many stars in one place. Pierre Lotti, the flamboyant house manager in his white tuxedo with his inseparable budgie on his shoulder, was determined to milk it for all it was worth.

On a small table by a white piano, Dalí was sitting with his habitual bottle of pink champagne. He didn't drink it himself. Just dipped his little finger in the glass and offered it to the members of his entourage. Aside from the eternal Gala, tonight that entourage included the Vietnamese transexual Amanda Lear – by then almost one of the family – and Mick Jagger who had come to visit Dalí in Port Lligat.

Jagger, who was wearing a white frilly shirt (*Beggars' Banquet* style), had already lost two things that day: Keith Richards, and the leather jacket he'd worn at the murderous Altamont gig.

He had unwillingly given it to Dalí as a gift.

Unbeknown to Jagger, Richards was actually partying incognito in a nearby candlelit corner with Gianfranco and Luca who were toying with some sugar cubes soaked in LSD. They had sold a batch to the hippies in Port Lligat the day before and were now feeling free and flush. Delighted to know themselves, they were giving the stuff away.

On the wall behind them hung a signed photo of Kirk Douglas looking sheepish with his dimple. He had been here a couple of years before. That had been a quieter night.

Lotti walked over to Dalí's table and asked him, first name terms, if he'd mind painting live, in front of everybody.

Dalí stood up ceremoniously and clapped his hands. 'Bring me a broom and some paint.'

It looked like a spontaneous event but actually the two men had talked about it previously. Dalí had agreed, on the condition that it was done on paper and the work was immediately binned after the event. Lotti thought he'd spring a fast one and exchanged the paper for a white tablecloth. He figured it would be worth something to someone, somewhere, someday.

Dalí didn't say anything. He just dipped the broom in the bucket and began to dramatically slosh paint over the tablecloth. Shouts of '*Olé*' and '*Bravo*' rang out around the bar. Among the audible intakes of breath, you could hear the occasional laugh and the clinking of glasses.

The whole bar was enthralled. All eyes were on the Great Masturbator as he held court. All eyes that is, except for those of the insatiable Gala who was busy drinking in Amanda, and a small group of noisy locals sitting at the bar chatting to an old man who looked like an ageing James Cagney in a dogtooth trilby.

The old man, who was wearing an open Hawaiian shirt which revealed a small blue butterfly tattoo, was telling them the long shaggy dog story that he'd told a million times of how he escaped from the infamous French penal colony of Devil's

Island by making a raft from a bag of coconuts and riding out on the tide.

It was Henri Charrière, the author of *Papillon*, a book which had been immortalised on screen by Steve McQueen that same year. Charrière had been in town for a while and the men had heard the story a dozen times. But it didn't matter. It was a good story and they would hear it a dozen times more.

These were the same bunch of locals who had ignored James Mason a decade before. He had been in Cadaqués filming *Les Pianos Mecaniques* (in English, *The Uninhibited*), the poster of which was hanging on the wall at the end of the bar.

Unlike Douglas or Jagger, his presence in the village had been met with such indifference he later sacked his publicity manager in a hissy fit.

Invisible to most of the locals or the jet set, Henri François Rey, the author of the novel which had inspired that film, was sitting at the table just in front of Richards and the Italians. Now a regular visitor, tonight he was drinking alone. Anis. And taking notes for his forthcoming book *Dalí Dans son Labyrinthe*.

He looked up from his paper. There was a round of applause as Dalí put the broom back in the bucket, bowed and said, '*Voila*,' pointing to a vaguely identifiable female figure on the tablecloth.

Lotti then turned to Jagger and asked him if he'd be so kind as to continue the show with a song. This hadn't been agreed previously. Dalí smiled and egged him on, 'I have performed and now, surely, it is your turn...'

On cue, the band which had been quietly getting into place while Dalí was performing, now began the chords of

'Satisfaction'. It was a set-up, but Jagger was soon strutting and singing. The whole bar went wild.

Lotti couldn't believe the night he was having. He felt like he was making history.

Nobody noticed the fight which broke out between a couple of English alcoholics over some beautiful girl who didn't understand what they were saying. Or the two Italians and the famous guitarist spellbound by the rivers of blonde candle wax pouring out from the wine bottle on their table.

At about the same time, Salva the bouncer was gently guiding a tall dark man with a 12-inch beard, a floppy hat and a copious number of beads, out of the bar and back into the night. He was being ejected for not consuming.

The man, who was in his mid-thirties, looked vaguely familiar. Maybe he was famous. Maybe he wasn't. Salva had received no special instructions. The man could have been another well-off northern European hippy or one of those freeloaders from the island. Either way, it didn't matter. The rules were the rules. No drinking. No staying.

Especially tonight with the star-studded spectacle that was going on inside.

The man didn't protest. He just ambled out into the warm air and wandered over to the pebbled beach where he lay down and listened to the muffled din of music, shouts and laughter floating up over the bay.

Then, he stood up, took off his sandals and let the silver water lap gently at his feet before deciding to go all the way. He slowly stripped off, put his beads in his hat and ran his fingers through his hair.

George Harrison was going for a midnight swim.

If he had looked back across the beach to L'Hostal, he would have seen a short stocky man leaving the place with paint-splattered tablecloth folded under his arm, whistling 'I can't get no Satisfaction'.

It was Dalí's handyman.

Lotti looked on wistfully from the doorway. His tux shining in the moonlight. The budgie blinking.

'Oh well,' he thought, 'at least I'll have tonight.'

They could never take that away from him.

> The sun hangs over the bay like a disco ball,
> the sea is full of golden sequins.

August 27.

Zigzagging

It seems like the population of the village has halved.

Yesterday, a steady trail of traffic began snaking up the hillside after lunch and headlights were still illuminating the hairpin bends long after the waiters – end-of-season tired – had cleared away the tables in the empty restaurants below.

This morning the village looks like a reimagined Hamelin. The parents have fled, leaving their children to be tended by an assortment of grandparents or helpful friends. The Piper, in this case, is wearing a suit. The tune is Money.

In the days before the Piper got two workers for the price of one, it was the Dads who would leave the kids and the wives in the village. This practice, sometimes referred to as doing a 'Rodríguez', comes from the time when the news was in black and white, Dad only had two weeks off and the school holidays lasted three months. Mr Rodríguez was in town on his own.

These days, we have Netflix. Mum and Dad both work. They have four weeks off, and the school holidays last almost three months.

There is still a shortfall.

Good job Spain has the longest life expectancy in Europe and the grandparents can babysit.

Shame the retirement age is 67.

194

In among that trail of traffic was the 5pm bus to Barcelona. The same bus that had brought our son, Tadhg, was now carrying Monica back home.

La Señora Rodríguez has left me behind with the kid.

Tadhg has escaped for a short visit between shifts at the Ramen restaurant where he's working between life choices. I don't see as much of him as I'd like. In Barcelona he seems to be asleep when I am awake, and I seem to be awake when he's asleep. So, it was good to get in a G&T at Cafe Tropical's Twenties' night.

Pep's daughter Naia, also working between life choices, has been hassling us to go all summer but it wasn't until I had the excuse of entertaining my own 20-something that I felt safe enough to venture into the world of plastic palm trees, sequins and mirror balls.

In the '60s and '70s, Cadaqués' nightlife was legend. Absolute scenes. The *Gauche Divine* would hit the town every summer and the epicentre of this nocturnal *Dolce Vita* was L'Hostal. A place where Mick Jagger and the King of Spain might rub shoulders while Dalí was signing napkins.

L'Hostal is now a touristy restaurant on the front and the golden years have gone the way of David Bowie. What glitter Is left is mainly restricted to cocktails in Brown Sugar, La Havana or Anita Nit MF. The debauchery is down at Can Shelabi. Meanwhile, La Frontera, Shadows Disco and Cafe Tropical cater for a less exclusive Northern European clientele whose shine is mostly due to an excess of sun.

When we arrived, the place was deserted. The sound system was blasting out some kind of techno Charleston. Naia was dressed in a skimpy vintage maid's outfit, along with the other six waitresses. They all seemed over-excited and scatty, as if acting out their costumes. Naia berated us gently for not having dressed up. We could have had a free shot.

The goldfish bowl G&T was enough.

Enough to loosen our tongues a little. But the conversation was, if not cagey, more guarded than I would have liked. Ever since Tadhg came back into the family home after four years in London, we have had to move around each other carefully, like the crabs in Cala Culip, lest the complications of expectation and fulfilment spark a conflict.

He's sensitive and I don't know when to shut up. It's like trying to negotiate those hairpin bends up on the hillside with the added difficulty that I don't drive, and sometimes I feel I'm too old to learn.

JC in prison pending trial, 319 days.

August 26, 2018

Nice ride down? I told you the maddo was on holiday. Guess what...   18.33

...just got bit mini shock by something weird snorkelling   18.34

I saw this pink spiky looking shell under some seaweed decided to investigate. Very carefully I put my finger near it and got a pretty interesting shock. Pulled me little finger out and it had two tiny slices out of it! Went back to have a look and the fucker had gone. Tales from the deep...   18..34

Teach me to poke about where I'm not wanted   18.40

Vigila, you are looking after T, not the other way round!!!!!   18.43

Fatherhood

Watching your children do well
is to be again, yourself
as a child, the first time you realized
you had done something right
 but lacked the words
 to articulate the emotion.

Watching your children do badly
is to be again, yourself
as a child, some time after bed time,
catching your Dad
through the crack in the door
crying like a baby

and wondering uncertain
whether, or not.

Autumn

Us with Us

Hippy Island

Immortalized in his innumerable paintings, the island of Port Lligat and its smaller sister island Sa Farnera sit just across the bay from Dalí's house.

Occasionally, at dusk and out of season, you can see wild boar swimming across the shallow water to eat the seagulls' eggs. Centuries before it might have been cows. Back then, the cowherds used the island for pasture. During the 1970s, the hippies were the ones doing the paddling.

Possibly inspired by Tangerine Dream singer Edgar Froese's visit to Dalí in 1966, or by the films *Los Pianos Mecanicos* (1965) and *The Lighthouse at the End of the World* (1971) – both of which were filmed in the area – in the 1970s, the star children descended on the place in force.

The island of Port Lligat became a kind of makeshift commune. It was known as Hippy Island.

The locals were not amused.

A newspaper at the time, *Los Sitios*, while careful not to insult them, said they were 'not good tourists, they are not convenient for our beaches, especially in Cadaqués which is a place for select holidaymakers and people of a certain standing'. The Gerona newspaper went on to recommend that 'the number of hippies be limited to avoid contamination from their pernicious habits and customs'.

Nothing happened.

Perhaps Dalí's indirect approval for the out of the ordinary, Gala's fondness for long-haired beautiful boys, or simply Spain's desire at the time to be seen as an open and welcoming destination for Europe's arty middle class (ergo its dropout sons and daughters), led to inertia. Hippy Island survived for over a decade.

Until 1986.

By then, the hashish had been replaced by heroin and the language of the Press had hardened. They were no longer hippies. Now they were 'undesirables', 'tramps', 'troublemakers' and 'drug addicts'. It wasn't long before the combined pressure of local businesses and neighbours forced the authorities to expel them from the island.

Nowadays, these eight hectares of balding island are mostly empty. For the curious tourists who want to visit its tiny beaches, there is an unofficial boat service which makes the fifty-metre crossing. Here, Juanito, ferryman and unofficial custodian of the island, takes people across in an old wooden boat for a couple of coins. Too shallow for oars, Juanito uses a rope to pull the boat across, it's a simple pulley system.

A bit of an oddball, Juanito. Enigmatic. It's not always easy to understand what he's saying, even if you speak the language. A slim, dark-tanned man with a sun-creased craggy face he looks a bit like he might well have been living on the island along with all those hippies.

It would be no surprise if he looked up at you through his bifocals and said: 'What should I have to tell you, oh venerable one? Perhaps that you're searching far too much? That in all that searching, you don't have the time for finding?'

The gull balancing on the chimney stack
is safer than the gull flying to the island.

— Cadaqués proverb.

September 2.

Glimpsing

The last warm Sunday evening on the terrace in Bar Estic. Effectively the last evening of summer, or the first of Autumn. There is no obligatory wait for a water-side table, the gin trolley is pushed up against the wall next to the main door, and Gaia is already animatedly talking about her winter plans for travel in Brazil and Colombia.

I suppose this is one of the huge differences between the Cadaqués of today and its previous incarnations: when the shutters come down, the youth leave town. In its previous versions – bastion against invasion, fishing village, vineyard or olive grove – the villagers either survived or migrated. You didn't escape hardship, you weathered it. Or ran for good.

These days, half the town disappears after the summer season and as the temporality and instant cash ethos of the tourist trade bites, the delicate balance between service and business will only get harder to maintain. The soaring cost of seasonal renting often means an apartment can fetch more for the month of August than a 12-month let.

Unless they make a serious effort to remedy the situation it's only a matter of time before the place sadly goes the way of Ibiza where this balance has already collapsed. There, many of the locals have been forced out by the spike in accommodation prices, and the temporary summer staff are forced to sleep in local gymnasiums. It is a Mediterranean museum resort for Northern Europeans. And an increasing number of Americans.

Yesterday I saw a couple of these Young Americans get caught out on the island of Port Lligat.

Monica and I had decided to go for an evening dip around the back of Es Caials where a narrow rocky inlet separates the island from the headland and Juanito operates his laid-back ferry service. There is no such thing as a timetable. He usually just packs up as the sun goes down. It's only about 100 metres from shore to shore and, if you are familiar with the crossing, there are parts where you can make it on foot.

The Young Americans weren't.

As we were getting ready to leave, we heard the shouts.

The two young Americans appeared on the opposite beach only to discover their ferryman was probably back at the Casino. If they had been travelling light they could have just swum for it, but they were carrying the sort of Harrod's picnic hamper you don't leave behind.

So we watched as gym-sculpted buzz-cut stripped down to his waist, held the hamper above his head and began to wade across, leaving his over-excited curly-haired girlfriend shrieking on the shore. With every metre, the water rose five centimetres until, inevitably, about a third of the way across it reached his chin and he turned back.

That was the deepest point. He could have carried on. Or they could have crossed easily 100 metres further up the inlet.

We waved goodbye and left them to it, sitting next to their hamper watching the big pink sun slip down behind the sloping olive groves around Dalí's house.

They were going to have a moment to remember. A story to tell for the next twenty dinner parties. Why would we take that away from them?

Tomorrow we'll be heading back to the normality of that other Mediterranean museum resort, Barcelona. And I fear the return.

What I'd give for an irreplaceable hamper and an impossible crossing right now!

There have been moments during this long summer sojourn when I have glimpsed another life. Its possibilities as endless as time irrelevant.

There has been no searching in guidebooks for bargain-basement five-star menus, no timetabled urgency, and no obligation. Either to work or to holiday.

And such quiet.

Such quiet.

If I were ever to live an ideal life, this summer would have been it. A swim, some lines, a slow lunch, a nap, a drink, some lines. Occasionally, love. Sometimes, a conversation.

Not so much a holiday, as a trip to the sanatorium in times of cholera.

JC in prison pending trial, 325 days.

Pyrene and Heracles in Cadaqués

All men have need of the gods – Homer

Gleaming with dentistry
they descended at the *Platja*
de Port Lligat. A head and a half
above the rest, they stood.

Contrary to legend
he was close cropped,
golden. She, with dark ringlets
gently. They glistened among us.

Brilliant in their aerial whites
they suggested ambrosia
and the asset-rich credibility
of a fully flossed future.

Then, I noticed his eyes
- a shade too close
for Deity. And she was
chewing, gum. Open mouthed.

Immense at first sight
I now believe them,
sadly, to have been
only Americans.

Festa Major 2018

Thursday September 8th

9h – Raising of the flag
Torre des Baluard de
l'Ajuntament

11h – Festival Mass

18h – Kids' Treasure Hunt
Passeig

19h – Ohio Big Band
Passeig

Friday September 9th

10h – Kids' drawing
competition
Passeig

12h – Foam Party
Under the bridge by the
Casino

22h – Havaneres with
Bergantí, Portdoguer

00:30h – Muntband
Orchestra , Passeig

Saturday September 10th

10h – Swim across the Port
– Platja del Ros

12h – Slippy log
Moll de Portdoguer

18h – Giants, *Dolls* racing
and Tug of War.
Passeig

23:30h – Festival Concert
with the Tapeo Sound
System + DJ
Passeig

Sunday September 11th

24th Walk to Cap de Creus
8h – Registration (Passeig)

20h – Sardanes with la
Cobla la Principal from
Banyoles
Passeig

21:30h – Fireworks
Passei

Two papier mâché giants are dancing in the main square.
Both are over 12 feet tall.
The man is carrying a hoe and a fishing net.
His name is Abdon.
The woman, a shade taller, has a green water jug on her head.
Her name is Lídia.
Of course it is.

September 10.

Singing

Well, that wasn't too bad. I didn't even notice the days in between. And here I am. Again. Back to back. Back with my back to the Bar Estic. Another evening back in the pink.

Yep, they kept my bar open for an extra week. Of course they did.

It's party time and the village has got its glad rags on. It's the *Festa Major.*

This morning I watched a steady trail of kids trying to walk along a greasy pole jutting out from the quayside in Port Doguer. They were trying to grab the yellow plastic duck sitting at the end of it. Not one of the skinny little figures made it. But they just kept on clambering up, slipping down and coming back. There was something of the Whitewalkers about them, the way that there seemed to be a continual and infinite supply of bodies prepared to sacrifice themselves for no logical objective and with a complete disregard for pain.

A few hours later, their parents were in the main square for their own particular cup of fun: a tug of war and the traditional village *doll* race. If you think it's weird to watch groups of

208

grown men arguing over a piece of string, imagine them running about with jugs of water on their heads. *La cursa del doll* involves contestants balancing a water urn – the *doll* – on their head for 100 metres.

These relatively small, flat-based amphoras used to be the norm in the village for everybody who didn't have access to their own well. That was most people right up to the early 1950s.

Strange they had electricity years before proper plumbing.

Stranger still they didn't use their hands to stop the jug from falling off their heads.

Come to think of it, they probably did.

I'm sure today's shenanigans are just a modern development to generate egg-and-spoon race mirth. And it works.

Everybody was laughing and drinking on first name terms. Except us of course. Sure, we were laughing and drinking but ten months on and we are still in the wardrobe among the coats. On first name terms with ourselves.

Any hope Monica ever had of becoming a member of the Narnian Cair Paravel aristocracy has always been an ascent littered with obstacles. The main obstacle being me. Gently squeezing her hand under the table at the bar. Stay. Look. Watch.

But she was born for days like these. For balancing pots on her head and drinking wine from a leather pouch and possibly watching her husband bang his head on a greasy pole. For getting involved. She drinks community spirit like cava. These are her people and that is her flag. The one over there hanging from the top of Es Baluard. The enormous *Estelada*. A flag so

209

big that on a clear day you can see it from Civitaveccia. So big you can see it from Madrid.

Last night it rippled in the moonlight as we sat on the beach in Port Doguer and listened to the typical *havaneres* and drank toasted hot rum. I burnt my lip on a stray coffee bean floating on the top of the fiery liquid.

These maritime tunes, sung in a vaguely barbershop quartet style, go back to the days when people were emigrating to Cuba. And yes, they have a special resonance here in Cadaqués.

When they finished singing *El Meu Avi* (My Grandpa), half the people on the beach began to chant '*Llibertat Presos Politics*' (Free the Political Prisoners). I chanted too. With *gusto*. For politics I'm prepared to come out of the wardrobe.

But the chanting wasn't as unitary as you might think. When the kids next to us began to join in – they must have been about eight or nine years old – their Dad quickly told them to shut up and asked (in Catalan) 'what would you know about it?'.

'We know plenty,' they replied. 'Everybody shouts it in the playground.'

The lyrics of *El Meu Avi* refer to a warship, *El Català*, which was sunk during the Cuban war of 1898 and in which all sixteen crew members who drowned came from the same Catalan village: Calella de Palafrugell. Just down the coast.

El Meu Avi is considered a national symbol. It is a signifier. Another one.

The last day of the Cadaqués' *Festa de Major* is Tuesday. September 11th. *La Diada*. The national holiday of Catalonia. On that day in 1714 they lost their umpteenth war against Spain.

210

The party will end the same way it began yesterday morning, with Valencian firecrackers. The loudest bang known to man.

We'll be back in Barcelona by then, though.

As long as there are no idiots blocking the motorway, protesting about prisoners.

JC in prison pending trial, 330 days.

September 15, 2018

Where are you? La Roca? *13.04*

Vallgorguina. FFS *13.11*

Vallgorguina?! Is it the mad driver? *13.12*

Yep. But it's worse than that *13.13*

My worst kind of nightmare *13.13*

A lorry turned over and has blocked the road. So, I guess I won't be there till late. *13.13*

And I need a poo.... *13.14*

211

> I heard the woman next to me speaking Spanish,
> I turned to ask her the time, in my best Catalan,
> *'Perdoni, sap quina hora es?'*
> She replied, heavily accented, *salat*:
> 'One quarter and five of the one,'
> It took me 20 minutes to work it out.

September 16.

Mutating

Monica sleeps. Early Sunday morning and I have just returned from a very skinny dip in a deserted Pera Fet. And I needed it. A reward for the hell of yesterday's six-hour journey to get here. Thanks to an overturned lorry I missed half my weekend. I could have gone to Delhi in the time it took to travel those 100 miles. It caused more disruption than a group of angry republicans.

Pera Fet was so still and silent when I arrived that as I entered the water, I felt like the first person to walk on snow. Ever. Those first ripples seemed so dramatic. So definitive, circling out across a flat and infinite sea. And yet, when I came out and looked back there wasn't a single mark left on the surface. Save for a couple of tiny bubbles which soon disappeared, the transparent skin of the sea had closed over. No footprints.

It was as if I'd never been there.

Back home, on the patios below our apartment, the kids' inflatable swimming pools have disappeared and dry leaves pile

212

up in the corners. For most of the second-homers, summer is definitively over.

It's as if they had never been here.

Unsurprisingly – possibly fortunately – nobody has told the tourists. The village is still half busy.

Most of them are middle-class early-retiree Brits. The ones who look like they might need to downsize to free up the housing market for younger families. There's a sprinkling of Scandinavians and refreshingly few French. But it's precisely at this time, the dusk between Summer and Autumn, when you can see how clearly tourism has supplanted all other forms of income for the villagers.

First, they were fisherfolk and battlers against the Moors, then winemakers with a merchant navy, then survivors in hard times, eking out a living from the olive groves, smuggling and the occasional patronage of great painters. Now they are waiters.

Actually, that's a bit harsh. Most of the *pota negras* are now owners: either of the apartments that are rented out, or the restaurants, or the bakeries, or the tourist boats. The majority of the waiters are from out of town. Some from as far away as Bolivia and Ecuador.

Everyone is better off.

Materially.

But I can't help wondering if I'm experiencing the fourth mutation of the village. And possibly its final death? Virtually wiped out by the pirates, economically ruined by the Phylloxera, frozen out by a surprise frost... will it now die, a victim of its own success?

The salty local dialect is already on the way out.

Yesterday I was watching a kids' birthday party in Poal. The children of the *Cadaquesencs* were running about with the kids of what the Catalans call the *nou vinguts*: the newly arrived.

Immigrants. Like me. And they were all screeching to each other. In Spanish. Not Catalan. Never mind *salat*.

That is how a language dies. Not by crudely enforced diktats from nasty central governments but by kids being nice and wanting to talk to each other in the playground.

And there's me thinking the village motto *nos amb nos* still held true.

It certainly won't last very long if no one can say it anymore.

Lately, I've seen the slogan sprayed on a couple of walls. Seen like that, this 'us with us' in all its naked crudity comes across as another reactionary right-wing slogan. Another populist kickback against the ills of globalization. It might as well read 'Cadaqués First'.

Its variant, *nos per nos*, us for us, isn't much different and still reeks of insularity. But both versions claim to refer to the spirit of a people that built 2,000 kilometres of dry-stone walls to cultivate the eroding hillsides with vines: a spirit of co-operation and determination in the face of adversity. Looking after each other. Looking out for each other. And encouraging each other to marry local.

They'll have needed that motto back then. Half the women went bald and lost their teeth from carrying those rocks on their heads.

As for this *vell vingut*, for the time being I'm happy to be here taking full advantage of this autumnal Cadaqués. Playing my part in its downfall. Or its salvation. (Depending on where I'm sitting and what I'm drinking.)

Perhaps this is the future we are all destined for. Weekend escapes for the masses to impeccably beautiful museums full of ghosts and haunted by the echo of dead languages.

Places where socks in sandals are common but at least the women still have their hair.

JC in prison pending trial, 339 days.

Lilac wine

Chris, a swarthy late-fifty-something hasn't changed his style since The Clash brought out 'London Calling'. Originally from the flatlands of the fens, I find him sitting on the jagged top of Cap de Creus in his restaurant.

His doctorate in genetics is ancient history now. He's guarded, distant. A bit of a topic hopper. Odds-on he's a stoner or an ex-stoner. He occasionally breaks off mid-sentence and looks out across the cape. Into the Mystic.

On the other side of the building, one of his protégés, Toby, is plugging in his amp for this evening's session of down-at-heel anguish on top of the world.

Chris arrived in Cadaqués in 1991 after a stint working in Barcelona's legendary London Bar with its live music, absinthe and ladies of the night. He might have served me a beer back in the day.

The Cap de Creus restaurant was a half-ruined, unintentionally non-profit organization for lost souls when he took it over. It now makes a profit. On a good day, the takings might be as much as 10,000 Euros. It is the perfect galleon for this pirate from the lowlands.

He has owned the freehold now for almost two decades and in true *Cadaquesenc* tradition, has married into the village and invested in another project. His wife is the daughter of the owner of the Gritta, known as The Bug. The project is Can Shelabi.

Chris says Shelabi was the name the Moroccans (who ran the bar before) used to call a 'man who lived off women'. Not so much in the pimping sense. Just taking advantage. A quick online search has the name down as Egyptian in origin. Spiritually intense. Able to sting or charm.

It doesn't matter. Most nights, the passage outside Can Shelabi smells like the Rif Valley. Inside, the atmosphere in the bar harks back to the headiest days of the London Bar. But make no mistake. It's not L'Hostal. There's nobody in a tux running the show.

And Cadaqués has changed. When Damien Rice recently passed through, he didn't come in for a drink, leaving behind a good story and possibly a black-and-white photo. When he performed his impromptu song for the crowd, it was in the exclusive lounge of the upmarket boutique hotel Villa Gala. 400 Euros a night. Hung the video on YouTube. Four million hits. Times change.

Can Shelabi is more tattoo than tuxedo and it has a bit of a reputation for *trapicheo,* as the locals call it: somewhere you might score drugs. The late-night jam sessions can be chaotic. You get the feeling that the local authorities would probably like to have closed it down but probably didn't get it together.

Possibly too busy hanging flags on the lampposts.

Sweet and heady.

It is Lilac wine.

> Out of it man, and in the mood
> for the Can Shelabi blues, oh yeah
> the Can Shelabi blues

October 7.

Naming

The tiniest of coves. Hidden away near Poal with spikily difficult access and beyond a sign which reads, 'Beware of falling rocks.'

It has no name. In reality, it's not a cove. Just a rocky inlet. But it is well protected from this morning's Tramuntana, which is handy because Autumn has arrived as abruptly as Summer began. The wind is no longer a welcome breath of fresh air but a stark warning. Winter is coming.

I woke up with two questions knocking about in the back of my mind. Firstly, is it valid, possible or honest to write about other people if you are a bit of a misanthrope? Secondly, if I am a bit misanthropic – and that is not a foregone conclusion – why do I get so irked about the Cadaqués *nos amb nos* attitude? After ten months coming here, the only people who I'm sure know our names are Pep, Mercè and Naia: the landlord, his wife and their daughter. I think Javi the painter knows my name. But not *our* names.

The answer may be slightly complicated and vaguely worrying. It's the chicken and the egg of emotional stereotyping. Does the kid who isn't allowed to be a member of the gang later become the sociopathic gun-toting murderer of the Columbine High School massacre because of his

218

rejection? Or was he harbouring those thoughts all along and just didn't join in?

Last night in Can Shelabi, the carnival was in full swing. The wild things and the washed-up rolled their terrible eyes and danced their terrible dance.

A vaguely promising concert by a hippy band with a Bayou kind of sound gradually morphed into an anarchic, noisy party. The decrepit pill-popping trust-fundees and local dope fiends were dancing away to the early hours. *Pulp Fiction* style.

Sitting in the passage outside in a fug of weed smoke (not mine) and being ignored or ignoring (chicken/egg), despite having coincided with many of these same people in a lot of these Bacchanalian events, I finally discovered the name of one of the regular freaks who visit the bar.

Until then we had always referred to her as 'the lady of the laugh'. But it turns out that this junky-thin woman with the brunette bob, dressed in Chanel, glass of white wine accessory, dances like Uma Thurman in the diner scene, is called Jonah-Lee. Jonah fucking Lee.

I am not making this up.

You might not need to know someone's name to love them, but I think at that moment, as someone called out hers, I loved her just a little bit more. Jonah-Lee.

She came outside and stood next to Maria, the self-proclaimed Swedish gipsy princess, who was sitting alone, shipwrecked and vaping at a small wooden table. I had talked to Maria a couple of times in her gallery but there was no recognition last night. She was too far gone to recognize or remember.

219

Jonah-Lee tuned towards her, although I think she was addressing the whole crowd, and shouted out in plummy South African English (does that accent even exist?): 'Daaaaahlings daaaarhlings. Doooo come inside, there's fun to be had. There's music and dancing and plenty more...'

Then she swirled back into the bar, laughing that laugh that falls somewhere between a self-conscious Prom queen and a horse on cocaine.

The gipsy princess was unmoved and stayed at the table looking down into her empty glass, breathing huge clouds of steam out of her nose and into the gloom.

I went back in to dance with Monica.

Nobody knew our names.

We went wild.

JC in prison pending trial, 360 days.

Can Shelabi

Number 42 of 92 restaurants in Cadaqués

Vikram
NewDelhi   **'Over the rainbow'**

👍 08

Maaaan. Go to this place and give everybody a hug, hug yourself, hug your friends, and especially the barman. He really knows how to have a good time. He drinks with you, dances with you, he keeps the place alive. This is not a touristy place, its more for the locals. And that is the best thing. Wanna get drunk and dance with the locals, go here. Wanna watch a match, go here. I saw *El Classico* here. The crowd, the waiters, everybody was like one giant organism twisting and turning in sync. One heartbeat. Once again, thank you. Love on you. Hope we meet again soon. Over the rainbow.

Date of visit: September, 2018

Open embrace, closed embrace

Tango, the dance of goodbyes, emerged from the shadier port areas around Buenos Aires and Montevideo towards the end of the 19th century. Exactly the same time the *Cadaquesencs* were escaping the devastation wrought on the village by the arrival of the Philloxera.

Drawn to the Americas and Cuba in their hundreds, Catalan immigrants were accompanied by other Europeans in search of El Dorado, especially Spaniards, Czechs, Poles and Italians. In the port area of Rio Plata, they mixed in the bars and brothels with the Creoles and the freed African slaves. From this melting pot came the fusion of music and dance that Borges once described as 'horizontal desire you do vertically'.

Like Cadaqués, the origins of its name provoke fierce dispute, but the argument only reflects the diversity of its roots and adds to the mystique. The historian Rodrigo Rodríguez claims the word 'tango' comes from a language brought by slaves from the Congo and referred to the word for 'meeting place'. Others say it came from a Nigerian word for the God of thunder, *Shango*. More mundane explanations refer to the Portuguese *tanger*, to play an instrument, or the Spanish *tambor*, drum.

Shango, *tanger* or *tambor*, it's not hard to picture the scene around 1893 in a dusty warehouse, a few miles from the port in Buenos Aires and close to the old covered market, as Tendy and Riya, originally from Cape Verde are locked in a close embrace. Honza, from Bohemia, and Carlo from Genoa, sit on upturned tobacco crates drawing out a mournful tune on their accordion and violin. In the corner, Bernat who has recently arrived from Cadaqués via Cuba, adapts the words of a popular *havanera* and begins to sing what was later to become that 'sad thought you can dance to'.

It wasn't long before the warehouse became known as a hot spot for this newly created mestizo sound and the place soon morphed into the Bar 12 de Octubre, a name which is either an ironic coincidence or an intentional nod to the date of Columbus' arrival in the Americas.

Now known as El Boliche de Roberto and still a hugely popular haunt for tango lovers in downtown Buenos Aires, Bar 12 de Octubre is one of the earliest recorded venues for the genre.

The Cadaqués Tango festival takes place every year on the second weekend of October.

This year it falls on the 12th.

Quien sabe si supieras
que nunca te he olvidado
volviendo a tu pasado
te acordarás de mí…

October 13.

Endings

Are always too slow a dance.

Huge clouds brood over El Pení and the slate green sea murmurs winter in the bay. No matter how hard I try, thoughts of our imminent goodbye invade every step I take. We are locked into the closed embrace of our last dance.

This morning, walking in Caials with Monica, looking over to the island of Port Lligat – deserted except for a small *Estelada* someone had planted on the tiny beach – I just kept thinking, 'this isn't it, it's not quite right, the picture is spoilt.' The incongruous houses built so close to the water, ruining the view, smudging the canvas. The sad grey sea fret making a swim uninviting. All the cars parked anywhere. The people milling about, almost a crowd.

Why did they bother me then? They had been there the whole time.

I seem to have banished the joyful concept of the year of the lilo and encased myself in a tomb of leavings. As a result, the OCHD has kicked in hard and the song has gone wrong. I'm eliminating the positive, accentuating the negative: a self-defence mechanism that comes into force when I can see the end of something.

By focusing on the niggles, I dull the sharp pain of departure. Then, irritated by the imperfections, impatience sets in. I want to hurry everything along. Put the finality with all its suitcases on the train as quickly as possible. No messing about.

Leaving is not such sweet sorrow. Leaving sucks. Even when the village itself seems to be playing the alluring part of the mournful lover, waving goodbye through the clouds of smoke on the platform.

Last night, there were tango dancers on the terrace of the Casino and as the powerful floodlight threw their enormous graceful shadows of melancholy across the façade, I wondered – again – just how often it has felt that the village and myself seem to be in some kind of symbiotic relationship.

We didn't know about this weekend's festival and yet there we were looking up at nostalgia's muse, listening to some South American crooner over the sound system:

'Who knows if you knew
I have never forgotten you
returning to your past
you'll remember me...'

Who programmed that coincidence? What telluric magic made her offer us such a wistful goodbye?

Oh, Cadaqués. You're breaking my heart.

JC in prison pending trial, 366 days.

October 17, 2018

www.theguardian.com/world/2019/mar/
24/custo-costa-brava-hotel-plans-sa-
guarda-Cadaqués   *11.04*

Says they can't stop it cos they got all
their *permissos* in order   *11.04*

Diners *fastigosos* !!!!!   *11.08*

Time to leave huh?   *11.09*

Scotland here we come…   *11.16*

As long as we don't have to go
there in the coach with the mad
bus driver!!   *11.18*

Bad blood

What is a civil war if not a fight to the death between neighbours?

Despite its vaunted *nos amb nos* ethos, Cadaqués was not immune to the internecine conflict of the Spanish Civil War. Worse still, it was not immune to the civil war within the civil war that raged so virulently in Catalonia.

From the beginning of the war in 1936, there were two prison camps established in Cadaqués. One in the church, the other on the land where the swanky Playa Sol hotel now stands. Both were run by the pro-Republican side. The legitimate government.

Roughly speaking, up to this point, there had been an *entente cordiale* between the different factions fighting against the Fascists in Catalonia. They were Republican. They were Catalan. Anyone who didn't tick at least one of those boxes ran the risk of ending up in one of those camps.

But in May 1937, a couple of the factions decided to aim for twisted ideological purity and added a couple of extra boxes: the economically powerful and the ideologically suspect. The last one was a particularly arbitrary category. Things quickly turned sour and infighting broke out between anarcho-syndicalists, communists and socialists.

As George Orwell said in *Homage to Catalonia:* 'it was a horrible atmosphere produced by fear, suspicion, hatred, censored newspapers, crammed jails, enormous food shortages and prowling gangs.'

And those were the good guys.

On May 6th, 1937, the bad blood arrived in Cadaqués. And there was no shortage of aggrieved locals willing to don the red-and-black beret of the CNT.

Against the wishes of many villagers, the militia had already unsuccessfully tried to burn down the church with anti-clerical fervour. Now they set their sights on anyone they considered ideologically suspect.

That fourth box.

And it included fellow Republicans.

They detained and shot Manel Rahola, a cousin of the famous Republican writer and thinker Carles Rahola who would be assassinated by Franco at the end of the war. Incredibly, and luckily, Manel's wound was only superficial and he survived to tell the tale. Unlike the village schoolteacher Lluís Tasis who didn't last the night.

In his testimony from the time, Rahola said: 'There was a rumour that 45 neighbours were in danger of being murdered. For this reason, the ones who thought they might be in danger and weren't affiliated to the CNT-FAI (the anarchists) decided to leave by sea, others went to the headquarters of the PSUC (the socialists), and the rest hid out in the sheds in the olive groves. In total, during that week, more than 100 people left. 10 were assassinated.'

And he continues: 'Out of respect for their families, who weren't to blame, I won't mention the names of the *Cadaquesencs* involved.'

Inevitably, things got even worse when Franco's Catholic Unitary National Territorials marched into town, victorious. Requisitioning houses from the villagers, installing Falangists into positions of power and encouraging collaboration. Of which there was plenty.

This time, many more villagers left for exile in fear of reprisals and those who stayed were subject to obligatory military service and strict obedience of the new rules. They were fined for not attending mass. Fined for speaking Catalan.

In his book *Cadaqués Autentic?*, Heribert Gispert describes a scene involving his friend's dad: 'One Sunday morning he met the boss of the Falange who fined him five pesetas for not attending mass. The poor guy couldn't believe it and said to him (in Catalan) 'Don't you think you're making a mountain out of a molehill?''

His answer was as quick and sharp as a slap in the face: 'Another five pesetas for not speaking Spanish."

The man imposing the fines was not only his neighbour, but a childhood friend.

They used to fish together.

Nos amb Nos eh?

> *Cap de grop* is a *Cadaquesenc* expression.
> It is used to describe the clouds that threaten an imminent storm.
> Figuratively speaking, a *grop* represents great difficulty.

November 1.

Fighting

All Saints Day or Day of the Dead. Traditionally, the day I and the boys have chosen as our name day. Us being a saintless and ungodly trio. There'll be no celebrations today though.

It has been raining an ocean's worth all week. Not just sweet water. Buckets of salty tears too.

Although it has now stopped, the clouds still sulk over the village and Monica is severely affected by a bout of low pressure. The combination of an unexpected family dispute, the inevitable ending to our time in the apartment (we have come with a van), and several dark days of Autumn storms.

When we arrived for the long weekend, groundwater was still flooding down over the hundreds of dry-stone walls holding up the mountainsides. For some reason, these hundreds of fountains and tiny streams trickling their way down to the sea reminded me of a Chinese gift shop. I just need to find a golden cat with a swinging arm to cheer Monica up.

She is furious. This was supposed to be the weekend of the *cosinada*, when all the cousins met together for the first time.

Her cousin Anna lives in nearby Ciurana, a small village near Figueres, with her five kids. This means Dylan and Tadhg have five cousins they have never met and who they could possibly marry with no ill-effects (how could they not be interested?). It also means that Monica has been planning on getting us together for this weekend. It was important.

She doesn't see Anna often and she was keen. Keener still, on the possibility of a family foursome, Monica and me, Tadhg and Dylan, the four of us all being together for the first time in the apartment in Cadaqués. Incredibly, after 11 months we have never coincided. Both sons have been here separately. This weekend was the final chance.

It was important.

Monica has a very bad relationship with her father. Well, let's say he has a bad relationship with her. Either way, he hasn't seen his grandchildren for fifteen years and Monica is always desperate to try and maintain some kind of contact with the saner members of the family. Weekends like this are a chance for her to feel that her family isn't a complete antithesis to the close-knit extended Iberian model.

It was important.

And it rained, and rained, and rained.

A couple of days before we were due to come, Dylan announced he was staying in Barcelona. Tadhg followed suit once he saw the weekend unravelling. The ins and outs weren't particularly complicated. They are 19 and 23 years old. Sometimes they misread things.

Monica was apoplectic. Not so much for the cousins but for the sons. Her immediate family is very much her *nos amb nos*. The resulting storm was Katrina huge.

After which, Dylan moped around like a mistreated puppy (his mum spoils him and he is unused to being shouted at). Tadhg was hyper-smiles trying to iron out the kinks in the cloth (he can't stand conflict and is over-sensitive).

231

Me? To be honest, I was as happy not to do the *cosinada* as I was to do it. I'll see the kids again on Sunday.

In a way, it's nice to have these last few days to myself to mull over this last year.

Also, perversely, I found the event somehow reassuring. Fighting? It happens in the best of families. I mean, look at the Dalís!

Blood is sweeter than honey.

JC in prison pending trial, 384 days.

October 31, 2018

Cheer up baby. At least we don't have to go on the bus... *11.04*

Humph. *11.08*

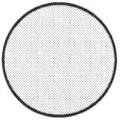

Can Rafa

Number 7 of 92 restaurants in Cadaqués

BFawlty
Torquay   **'Bad attitude'**

👍234

Booked a table for 4 at this restaurant on 19th sept and arrived and was seated by the owner. As we looked at the menu, a couple in their 60s arrived for a table they had booked for an anniversary, it seemed they had requested a certain table and when this wasn't available, they questioned it with the owners. He literally told them to take it or leave it, he was so rude and loud in front of all the customers to this extremely quiet and almost timid couple that we stood up and told him that because of his behaviour that we decided to leave. As we left, his father followed us out onto the street and kept repeating, bye bye, bye bye, bye bye, in a very loud and aggressive manner. The other couple also left.
This was probably the worst attitude I have ever seen in any restaurant ever. We were so shocked we left Cadaqués and went back to Roses to eat.

Date of visit: September, 2018

Fire on the water

Imagine a cold moonless winter's night at some unknowable point during the Dark Ages. A fisherman is sitting on the seashore by a fire grilling a sea bass he caught earlier that day. Nearby, in the water, he notices an unusual amount of activity. He picks up a branch from the fire and moves closer to look. To his surprise, below the reflection of flame on the surface, he sees the flickering shadows of fish. To his delight, as he moves the branch slowly from side to side, the flickering shadows move too.

Not quite the invention of the wheel but for that solitary angler, a definite Eureka moment. And for Cadaqués a spark that would light centuries of fires.

La pesca encesa, fishing by firelight or, translated literally, fishing alight, was an integral part of life in Cadaqués for generations. Plankton love lights. Anchovies love plankton.

In the early days, a fire of pine logs and olive branches would be lit in an iron grate that hung from the hull of an anchored boat known as the *llagut de foc,* the fireboat. Meanwhile, half a dozen men on another, larger boat would throw out the nets for the catch.

As time passed, the fires were replaced by oil lamps, kerosene and eventually, electricity.

Not all the coves around Cadaqués were equally productive, a good catch depended as much on the currents and the wind as on the fire and the men.

Cala Jugadora was particularly sought-after. The competition was fierce and by the 16th century, regulation was in force. Each cove was assigned to one crew for each season.

234

On good nights, when the sea was calm and the moon was new, as many as fifteen boats would be out.

Seen from high above, in the days when the land was still cloaked in darkness, the lights scattered around the jagged headland of Cap de Creus would have looked uncannily like a reflection of the night sky. A constellation of boats. Like the Carina, part of the Argo Navis constellation, identified in Greek mythology with the ship used by Jason and the Argonauts in search of the Golden Fleece.

A harvest moon rises over the bay. Amber ripples the surface.
On the horizon, embers glow. Orange sparks scatter upwards.
Someone is cooking on an open fire, out at sea.

November 17.

Encircling

We did it.

Almost.

Woke up to a miserable day of rain in the month of the drowned dog. But I was feeling surprisingly upbeat. The plan remained the same and it was today, or possibly never.

We got dressed, grabbed the brollies and set off. Monica walked a step or two behind me. I hadn't told her about the plan. Just asked her to stick with me and not ask too many questions. As we crossed the village, over the rain-soaked *rastell,* she complained cheerfully that I looked like a man who didn't know where he was going or what I was doing.

I'm pretty sure she knew what I was up to really.

It began to rain sideways, under the umbrellas and into our wellies and I'll admit I was having doubts. But once I arrived at the fish counter in the supermarket, I knew there was no going back.

Half a dozen sardines, a few prawns and an instant, easy-to-light barbecue tray.

We were going to Pera Fet. This was my Christopher Robin moment.

As we left the supermarket and walked along the *Riba*, past Picasso's old house and the boats in Poal, the rain teeming

236

down, I didn't need to look at Monica to know she was smiling sardonically at my gentle madness. I didn't care. I had been waiting for this moment since Spring.

The beach would be empty. The fire risk would be nil (everything was soaked, including us) and in the worst-case scenario, I was banking on the house of the ironic breakfasters being empty so we could use their porch.

In the end, we only needed their porch to leave the umbrellas.

The rain slowed. We put the barbecue tray in a corner at the end of the beach, set it alight and washed the fish in the sea. We were soon grilling away happily in the drizzle.

They didn't take long (a good thing I suppose, considering the weather) so we chucked some damp driftwood on the remnants of the barbecue to make a proper fire.

Bonfires are great. So practical and transcendent.

As the embers faded, we finished the feast. Our fingers sticky with scales and juice. It was grey and spitting. Threatening a storm again. The Cucurucuc rock was sulking out at sea like a humpback whale.

We washed our hands at the edge of the water and a sly wave caught Monica's boots, so she took her shoes and socks off. We revived the fire, hung the socks on a stick to dry, and huddled up next to the flames.

We kissed. Didn't say much. Didn't need to.

The beach was deserted. Winter was closing in.

Just us, with us...

... and a tatty plastic bag.

JC in prison pending trial. All this time.

Us with Us

Epilogue.

On October 14, 2019, JC (Jordi Cuixart) was found guilty for his part in the 'illegal' referendum. He was sentenced to 9 years in prison for sedition. His eight companions received similar, or longer, sentences. The former Catalan vice-president, Oriol Junqueras, was sentenced to 13 years.

In Cadaqués, members of the local *CDR* joined demonstrations to block the motorways. The restaurants closed, if only briefly, in protest. Most of them are closed on Mondays in October anyway. Many of the villagers held a small demonstration at the roundabout.

The weather was surprisingly mild – 24º C and sunny – but the *tramuntana fina* whispered winter down through the olive groves into the town, where thousands of yellow ribbons fluttered nervously in the breeze.

The mad bus driver? He took early retirement.

Us with Us

Glossary of Catalan words and phrases.

Barretina. Traditional Catalan red hat. Similar to those worn by gnomes.

Bon dia, com va, fins demà, ix! Good day, how's it going, aye!

Braves. Fried potatoes served with a spicy sauce.

Café solo. A small black coffee, although, strictly speaking, in Catalan, the *solo* is an unnecessary Spanish addition. A coffee is a coffee and a *café* is really just a *café*.

Caldo. Broth or stock.

Casa Blava. Blue House. This modernista house is currently up for sale. They are asking 22 million Euros.

Clopers. Small spherical piles of stones left by builders of the stone walls.

Cosinada. An invented word, from the Catalan *cosin*, cousin, to describe a meeting of all the cousins which, in this case, never happened.

Doga. A barrel. Typically used for salted anchovies or wine.

Diners fastigosos. Shitty fucking money.

Dolls. Water urns, like small Greek amphoras, for many years carried on the heads of the local women.

Empordà. The area in North East Catalonia in which Cadaqués is located.

Festa major. The yearly village party, usually with music, games and fun.

Festes. Parties or celebrations.

Gusto. A Spanish word meaning desire or taste, used here to express really wanting to do something.

241

Havaneres. Songs about the sea, usually sung in harmony and with a guitar or two, and perhaps an accordion.

Independentista. A person who believes that Catalonia should be an independent state.

Indians. The people who emigrated to South America at the turn of the 20th century, and sometimes returned to their native land to spend the money they had made.

La Lídia de Cadaqués. One of the village's most famous ladies. Despite her poverty, she became the subject of books and music, and was lauded by Dalí himself.

La mare que la va parir. An exclamation meaning damn the mother that gave birth to her, in context, more like, 'bloodyhell, what an asshole!'

Llibertat Presos Politics. Free political prisoners.

Lliure. Free.

Paella popular. A huge rice dish, paella, often cooked in the main square and shared between the locals. Sometimes as many as 100. Typical either in political events or popular celebrations like the annual village party.

Patocada. A dance, typical to Cadaqués, which involves hitting your dance partner in time to a chant, usually comic. The *patocada* is usually chanted by someone who is 'leading' the dance.

Penes. Sorrows.

Pepe Botella. The nickname for José I Bonaparte, briefly the King of Spain from 1808-1813, referring to his fondness for a tipple. *Botella* is Spanish for bottle.

Pernil. Cured ham

Porró. Traditional long-necked glass jug used for drinking wine in groups. It is held up at arm's length and the arc of wine is supposed to fall into your mouth. Inexperienced users often end up with stained clothes.

Pota negra. *Pota negra* is the best type of Spanish ham. In Cadaqués it is sometimes used to describe the locals who have the longest roots.

Procés. The term given to the interminable, and as yet unsuccessful, battle for the independence of Catalonia. Critics view it as a long-drawn-out propaganda war with little substance.

Salat. The local dialect of Cadaqués, literally translated as 'salty'.

Sardanes. Traditional Catalan dance, performed in a circle, sometimes of up to as many as 60 people. The dancers hold hands and gently bounce up and down in time to the music. The steps are mathematical and are usually spoken by a 'caller' in the circle.

Societat de l'Amistat. Before becoming a cultural centre for the village, la Societat l'Amistat had a different function. Founded in 1857 its role was to help the villagers. Directed exclusively by men, it acted in much the same way as today's social security system. Each member paid a monthly quota and in return got insurance in times of sickness.

Som Republica. We are a Republic!

Taps de Cadaqués. Traditional small sponge cakes made in the town, often served with rum.

Vell vingut. A play on words taken from the Catalan for *nouvingut*, which is newcomer, and often refers to immigrants. As someone who has been here for a while, I am an oldcomer. *Vell*, old.

Us with Us

Acknowledgments:

Thanks to Hannah Pennell, Mike Eaude, Matthew Tree, Stephen Burgen and Thomme Chandler for their encouragement and comments.

I'd also add that much of the historical information, sometimes embellished, would have been impossible without the help of Josep Pla's *Cadaqués*, the books of Heribert Gispert and Firmo Ferrer i Casadavall, Rafael Tirado's *Cadaqués de portes endintre* and the Raholas' ridiculously weighty *Marina Mercant de Cadaqués* which helped improve my Catalan no end.

Ryan Chandler is co-author of DK's *Top 10 Barcelona*, publisher of the literary magazine *Barcelona INK* and editor of the compilation of the series of the same name: *The Best of Barcelona INK,* Catalonia Press.

He lives and works in Barcelona.

Javier Aznarez is a well-known painter and illustrator. He runs the gallery Taller de Tabakov and recently worked on the animation for Wes Anderson's *The French Dispatch.*

He lives and works in Cadaqués

Printed in Great Britain
by Amazon